*Parenting a Child
with a Behavior Problem*

Also by Cheryl G. Tuttle and Penny Paquette

Thinking Games to Play with Your Child
Parenting a Child with a Learning Disability

by Cheryl G. Tuttle and Gerald A. Tuttle

Challenging Voices: Writings by, for, and About
People with Learning Disabilities

Parenting a Child with a Behavior Problem

A Practical and Empathetic Guide

Second Edition

Penny Hutchins Paquette
Cheryl Gerson Tuttle, M.Ed.

Foreword by Jefferson B. Prince, M.D.

LOWELL HOUSE

LOS ANGELES

NTC/Contemporary Publishing Group

Library of Congress Cataloging-in-Publication Data

Paquette, Penny Hutchins.
    Parenting a child with a behavior problem : a practical and empathetic
guide / Penny Paquette, Cheryl Gerson Tuttle : foreword by Jefferson B.
Prince.
       p.   cm.
    "Second edition"—Frwd.
    Includes bibliographical references and index.
    ISBN 0-7373-0256-0
    1. Problem children—Behavior modification. 2. Child rearing.
3. Parent and child. I. Tuttle, Cheryl Gerson. II. Title.
HQ773 .P36 1999
649'.64—dc21

                                         99-043084

Design by Mary Ballachino/Merrimac Design

Published by Lowell House
A division of NTC/Contemporary Publishing Group, Inc.
4255 West Touhy Avenue, Lincolnwood (Chicago), Illinois 60646-1975 U.S.A.
Copyright © 1999 by NTC/Contemporary Publishing Group, Inc.
All rights reserved. No part of this work may be reproduced, stored in a re-
trieval system, or transmitted in any form or by any means, electronic, me-
chanical, photocopying, recording, or otherwise, without prior permission of
NTC/Contemporary Publishing Group, Inc.
Printed in the United States of America
International Standard Book Number: 0-7373-0256-9
99 00 01 02 03 04 DHD 18 17 16 15 14 13 12 11 10 9 8 7 6 5 4 3 2 1

For Ben, Carlyn, Cameron, Sam, and Jared.

Contents

Foreword

All children (and parents) misbehave. In the second edition of *Parenting a Child with a Behavior Problem*, Cheryl and Penny offer thoughtful and practical guidance in recognizing behavior problems that affect our children.

As Cheryl and Penny say, children don't come with an instruction booklet. Most often parents develop a system that incorporates their experience with their philosophy on discipline. Frequently this is successful. However, even good children present with difficult behaviors. *Parenting a Child with a Behavior Problem* helps parents understand a variety of problematic childhood behaviors and foster an environment of positive development. Penny and Cheryl weave real-life anecdotes with ways of understanding, as well as parenting strategies, into a concise and updated guide. *Parenting a Child with a Behavior Problem* is appropriate for parents of children with the "normal" range of difficulties and those with more troubling and severe behaviors. Cheryl and Penny draw on their experiences, both personally and professionally, to create proactive parenting strategies that empower parents and families.

Parenting a Child with a Behavior Problem reviews common family, social, and school situations that both parents and children face. Penny and Cheryl help parents understand these situations from the child's perspective, as well as discuss the implementation of effective disciplinary strategies. They review ways for parents to effectively partner with their child's teacher to promote success at school. Furthermore, this book reviews a number of prosocial strategies designed to develop children's self-esteem and social capacities. Cheryl and Penny also discuss situations that may benefit from professional intervention. This discussion includes a review of psychological tests, which are used to assess children's cognitive capacities and emotional states, and the various classes of psychotropic medications prescribed to children.

Parenting a Child with a Behavior Problem is a timely and updated resource for parents. Cheryl and Penny have done an excellent job.

Jefferson B. Prince, M.D.
Co-Director, Anxiety Treatment Center,
North Shore Children's Hospital, Salem, Massachusetts

Acknowledgments

Cheryl and I would like to thank the many professionals—psychologists, counselors, teachers, administrators, and parents—who agreed to be interviewed. Without their cooperation, there would be no book.

We would like to especially thank Stephen McFadden, Dr. Ronna Fried-Lipski, Beth Viehman, and Libby Moore for sharing their expertise and resources.

A special debt of gratitude goes to Dr. Jefferson B. Prince for his review of the pharmacology section of this new edition.

Most of all, we would like to thank our families for their support and encouragement.

Introduction

"You're a jerk," six-year-old Samantha shouts at her mother. "You never buy me anything I want." Samantha's mother stares in disbelief. Never would she have spoken to her mother, or any adult for that matter, with such language or in such a tone. Where did Samantha learn such disrespectful behavior, her mother wonders?

Ten-year-old Ethan looks for ways to disrupt his teacher's lesson. When she asks him to "settle down" for the third time, he blows his classmate's work sheets onto the floor. He doesn't even try to conceal his amusement when his teacher loses her temper and sends him to the office. "I don't know why she sent me here. I didn't do anything," he tells the vice-principal.

Jessica comes into the house, runs up the stairs, and slams her bedroom door. Since the start of ninth grade, she has barely had two civil words to say to her parents. Now she frequently locks herself in her room. When her parents try to talk to her, she rolls her eyes with barely concealed contempt. She also steals money from their wallets to buy cigarettes they have forbidden her to smoke.

Parents, grandparents, teachers, psychologists, school counselors, talk-show hosts, educational consultants, in fact, most social observers acknowledge that the behavior of many children has deteriorated to an unacceptable level.

They are fresh. . . . They are rude. . . . They have no respect for other children, for adults, for property, for themselves. . . . . They have no value system, they have no morals.

That is what we heard when we told people we were planning a book on behavior.

Why are children behaving this way? People wanted to know. What has happened to cause this mess?

Is it television? Is it rock music? Maybe it's the movies, they said. Do video games have anything to do with it? Is it because so many mothers work? Is it because so many fathers are absent, they wondered? Is it because there is too little structure in our schools, or are our children's lives too structured? Is it because many families have turned away from organized religion? Have we overprotected our children? Have we demanded too much from them? Are our expectations too low? Do we pressure them too much? Should we feel guilty, or is it society's problem?

Wake up, Baby Boomers. Take notice, Generation X. As the cartoon character Pogo used to say, "We have met the enemy, and he is us."

Though we can probably attribute much of the decline in acceptable behavior to the negative changes in society, we must also acknowledge that as parents we are responsible for helping our children grow and develop despite society's negative influences. Society may influence our children, but we are the primary role models in our children's lives. Our children look to us for love, for guidance, and for stability.

We can't repair society all at once, but we can take responsibility for our homes and for our children. We can't expect others to do it for us. For now, we can't even be sure we will always get support outside our homes, but we can begin to make a change for the better. We can hold our children accountable for their behavior and in the process help them to grow into responsible adults.

We have written this book to help your children along in that process. Maybe you are concerned about your child's behavior. Maybe your friends, your relatives, your child's teacher, or activities advisor have complained about the way your child behaves. Maybe your faith in your instincts is beginning to fail, and you need some guidance. Maybe you just need to know you are doing the right thing.

Between us, Cheryl and I have raised five children and worked with thousands of others. We have talked to parents, teachers, child psychologists, school administrators, and counselors. We aren't behavior experts, and our research has assured us that no one has all the answers. But, like you, we are parents who want the best for our children, parents who want to see a positive change in the way today's children behave. We have collected anecdotes and strategies, advice and remedies, behavioral guidelines and developmental plans designed to help you develop a solid, predictable, reliable method of shaping or re-shaping your child's behavior. With guidance, you can take the steps toward change in your family.

Though as parents we might like to believe otherwise, no child is perfect. All children misbehave sometimes. Frustration, hunger, fatigue, temperament, fear, stress, peer pressure, and anger can all contribute to isolated incidents of poor behavior. That doesn't necessarily mean your child has a serious behavior or emotional problem. *Parenting a Child with a Behavior Problem* will help you recognize the imaginary line children cross that signals to us that something needs to be addressed and changed. It will help you understand when "crossing the line" is a normal part of development, when it can be caused by a specific incident or situation, and when a problem is more serious.

We have outlined normal developmental stages to help you understand what you should expect from your child as he grows into adolescence. With an overview of expected behaviors classified by age, you will begin to recognize your child's place on the continuum, and you will recognize when your child's behavior requires your attention.

Often, determining the cause of unacceptable behaviors is the first step in addressing behavior issues. We will help you understand why your child misbehaves.

When a child's behavior begins to disrupt normal activities, it creates a less than desirable emotional environment at home. Sometimes parents respond with anger; sometimes they feel guilty. Some parents feel sad or helpless. Others are frustrated. Occasionally parents deny there is a problem at all. *Parenting a Child with a Behavior Problem* will help you analyze and evaluate your feelings and will help you channel your emotions more productively. Specific discipline strategies will help you deal with your child's behavior problems in a positive way.

Often, children who are misbehaving have difficulty in school. *Parenting a Child with a Behavior Problem* will help you work with teachers, counselors, and administrators to make sure your child's behavior is not getting in the way of her academic progress.

Children with behavior problems often have difficulty in social situations as well. We offer some practical advice to help you help your child make and keep friends.

Once specific problems are under control, everyday strategies for success can be implemented. By fostering self-esteem, being a good role model, and avoiding old habits, you can help your child make good choices.

We present an overview of ethical development by recalling and reintroducing many of the guidelines our parents used when we were children. In this section, we help parents recognize their roles in the development of their child's character. We bid farewell to the attitudes of the "me" generation and present ways of helping our children learn to work and play in a cooperative and meaningful way.

For most parents, the ordinary behavioral problems discussed in the early chapters of this book are the most serious they will ever have to face. For many others, however, serious emotional problems or behavioral disorders will disrupt their children's lives and, in the process, turn their own lives upside down.

In chapter 7, "Getting Help," we provide an overview of behavioral and emotional problems that require professional help. This chapter will help you assess the severity of your child's needs. A list of typical symptoms for each of the disorders is included as well as current medical and psychological treatments for these serious behavior problems. The chapter also includes descriptions of the specific psychological tests and checklists that professionals use when evaluating children.

Although we have gathered information for this book from behavioral specialists, some of the best suggestions have come from parents just like you—loving, nurturing, understanding parents providing good role models for their children every day. Parenting is not an easy job, and society often presents roadblocks to successful discipline. But don't give up. If you believe, as do most experts, that parents are the most important influence on their children's behavior, you will accept the challenge and help your child grow into the kind of adult you respect and admire. The rewards for a job well done are the most gratifying imaginable.

CHAPTER 1

Getting Started

We've all been there. Some of us have nearly come unglued when our son or daughter threw a temper tantrum in the middle of the grocery store because we refused to buy candy or sugared cereal or a plastic toy. We have listened with a sense of disbelief as one of our beloved cherubs used an obscenity in a public place. Most of us have seen our children grab a toy from another child, or, worse yet, slug a classmate in the nose. Perhaps we watched in horror as one of our children pulled a chair out from under his brother. Or we might have received one of those less-than-welcome phone calls from the vice-principal at school. I once had one of *my* children say to *my* mother, "I hate your face!"

If you have children, you have probably been shocked by one of these unfortunate experiences. Behavior problems come with the territory. All children misbehave. Even though your best friend might like to believe her children are perfect, you know they aren't. Neither are yours, or mine, or Cheryl's.

When children are tired or hungry or bored or under stress, they are likely to act out. This type of misbehavior is entirely normal. Though this level of misbehavior is understandable, it is not acceptable. These situations require a response.

If we acknowledge that all children misbehave, then we must formulate a plan for those occasions when our children are less than perfect. If our child's misbehavior has escalated to the point where it is having a negative impact on the family, in relationships with friends, or in school, we need to take an active role in helping our child over these behavioral hurdles.

If we want our children to grow into the competent, caring, respectful adults we admire most, we must be involved.

As parents, we are responsible for instructing tomorrow's adults. Think about it. What job is more important than that? What we do today *will* affect the future. We are responsible for helping our children grow. We are responsible for instilling the moral values in our children that will help make the world a better place. When we take our job as seriously as we should, we recognize that our parenting skills need to be as solid as we can make them.

Most of us aren't born with an automatic pilot that takes over when we have children. When we were released from the hospital, no one handed us a "How to Raise a Perfect Child in Ten Easy Lessons" instructional video along with our bundle of joy. We get instructions with our major appliances, we take lessons to perfect our tennis serve or our golf game, we get on-the-job training at work on how to run the computer. But our only experience for parenting comes from remembering how our own parents did it. For most of us, our parents were excellent role models. For some, they were less than ideal. In either case, our parents raised children in a different atmosphere. Parents today face new and often more difficult challenges. Teachers, parents, and mental health professionals might argue over whether children's behavior has changed over the past generation. Few would argue that today's children are growing up in a different world.

When Cheryl and I were young, moms stayed home and dads ruled the roost. Our mothers did most of the instructing and disciplining, but final decisions were made by our fathers. They were *the* authority, and no one questioned authority. Most of us heard those dreaded words "Wait till your father gets home" more often than we care to admit. Times, as we say, have changed.

Nearly half the families today have working mothers. Many families are headed by single parents. Today, fortunately, more women's voices are heard and respected, and many fathers take a more active role in their children's day-to-day activities.

The war in Vietnam and the Civil Rights movement inspired many to question authority. What was once primarily an autocratic world is now a more democratic one. Our children are growing up in that world. For better or for worse, "Because I said so" just doesn't cut it anymore.

Today's children operate in a society that requires questioning, reasoning, critical thinking, and major decision making. When we make all of the decisions for our children, when we teach them to *always* listen to those in authority, when we tell them to obey *all* adults, we are doing them a disservice.

When we were children, our parents might have cautioned us to beware of strangers, but few of us had to decide whether that man who lost his puppy was someone who really needed our help or whether he could be someone who would hurt us. We might have faced the moral decision of whether or not to join an exclusive fraternity or sorority, but many of today's children must decide whether to risk independence or seek out the protection of a gang. When parents today were children, television choices ranged from *Little House on the Prairie* to *The Brady Bunch*. When your children watch television or use the computer, more realistic and often less wholesome choices abound. We need to help our children develop the skills to make more difficult decisions than most of us had to make when we were children. Our work is cut out for us.

Though our children need to be encouraged to question and to develop decision-making skills, that doesn't mean they are in control. That doesn't mean they have our permission to be rude or disrespectful. That doesn't mean they can decide to stay out all night if they choose, or elect to attend unsupervised parties. We are the parents. We are responsible for their physical and moral health and welfare. We can't abdicate that responsibility. Though we don't have to dominate with force, we are in charge. Children in today's turbulent, often out-of-control society need rules and structure more than ever. They need consistency. They need parents they can turn to when they have questions, and they need parents who can be good ethical role models.

Today's children need parents who can help them develop the confidence and abilities necessary to make good decisions, and they need dependable adults in their lives who are willing to say no when necessary. It *is* possible for parents to do both. Not only possible, but essential. Your children need you, and you need confidence in your abilities to guide your children. If you are interested in helping your child improve or simply want to keep your child on track, and if you love your child and want his behavior to reflect your standards, you are in a perfect position to raise a well-behaved child.

As simple as it sounds, many of the techniques of effective parenting and disciplining involve trusting your instincts. You have a goal for your child, and you want to achieve that goal while preserving your child's integrity and self-esteem. Though the task sometimes seems overwhelming, as parents we have what it takes to make positive changes.

Parenting involves loving, caring, nurturing, and teaching, but love alone is not enough. Simply loving our children will not guarantee our children will be well behaved. Though love provides an essential foundation, we need to build upon it with a well-thought-out discipline strategy, and we need to be firm in our resolve to follow through, even when the going gets tough.

Discipline strategies do not come in a one-size-fits-all package. You bring certain personality traits to your job as a parent. Your personality has been molded and modified over many years and is an important part of you. The strategies we discuss in this book will work for most parents and children in many situations; but keep in mind that no two parents and no two children are the same. You may need to modify strategies to fit your personality or your child's temperament. Find the strategies that work best for you and your family, and then stick with them. Consistency counts.

Corporal punishment doesn't work. It is true that as long as we are bigger than our children, we can force them to obey. Though it is sometimes comforting to believe our size and age are enough to command obedience, put us in control, and make us powerful, stop and think. Punishing our children may force them to obey, but what lesson have we taught them? Have we taught them what they have done wrong? Have we taught them what they should have done instead? Have we helped them learn to control their behaviors and to make better decisions? No. By example, we have taught them to control people with size and force, that "might makes right." What happens when we are not there to see their behavior? Will they make the kinds of choices we respect? What happens when an authority figure tells them to do something they shouldn't? Have we taught them to make a value judgment before acting?

When we punish, we don't teach. Discipline, however, is a teaching system that leads to orderliness and self-control. The way you teach discipline to your children helps them behave the way you want them to. When we discipline, we help children develop the skills required to make good choices.

Though our children are smaller than we are, it is a fallacy to think our children don't have any power. Our children have a great deal of power over our lives. Under most circumstances, when our children are happy, we are happy. When our children are sad or depressed, we suffer, too. Your child's mood can affect how you interact with your spouse, your coworkers, and your friends.

When children misbehave, many parents feel responsible. Sometimes they are. Though our children are precious to us and we love them unconditionally, when we neglect to teach them the difference between right and wrong we begin a cycle of behavior problems that can be difficult to overcome.

Parents who want to take control need to begin by formulating behavioral expectations. As parents, it is your job to set limits and make rules. The rules and boundaries must be flexible and grow as your child grows, and your child must understand the reasons for rules. When your family's rules are broken, consequences need to be predictable.

The strategies presented in chapter 3 are suggestions that have been provided by many experts. Behavioral specialists, child psychologists, pediatricians, school counselors, teachers, and parents just like you have developed effective strategies for parenting a well-behaved child. We have reviewed the best, added our personal bias, and present here a practical and empathetic guide to help your child over behavior hurdles.

Before you begin to develop your disciplinary plan, it is helpful to know why your child is misbehaving. Again, causes are not excuses for inappropriate behavior, but they will help you understand your child's way of thinking and will also help you choose the best discipline strategy for particular situations. Sometimes children are going through a developmental stage that makes their behavior more challenging. Sometimes a particular situation is causing them to misbehave. Problems at home can cross over and create problems at school. Just as often, problems at school create upsets at home. Occasionally, children suffer from emotional problems that require professional intervention.

The next chapter provides an overview of causes for children's misbehavior. Armed with this understanding, you will be in a better position to help your child modify her behavior.

When you begin examining the reasons behind your child's behavior, you are in control. This first step is crucial to your overall plan. Once you have made a commitment to change your child's behavior, you are on your way to a happier and more harmonious home.

CHAPTER 2

What Makes Children Misbehave?

Four-year-old Shira yells at her best friend and then intentionally knocks over the castle they built together. Eight-year-old Derrick just can't take no for an answer. Every issue becomes an argument. Ten-year-old Taylor is a wise guy. He loves to make jokes, usually at someone else's expense. None of us enjoys seeing these types of behaviors in our children, but if your child is typical, you will probably see all of them as your child grows and develops.

Remember the "terrible twos"? Most parents can identify with the phenomenon of behaviors that are typical of two-year-olds, when children seem to defy and fluster even the most tolerant parent. Just as there are predictable two-year-old behaviors, there are equally predictable behaviors normal to other stages of development. Behaviors may come on a little earlier or a little later with individual children, but with most children the pattern remains constant.

Behavioral experts have identified typical developmental stages for children, and despite certain variances, they agree upon a range of behaviors parents can refer to when trying to determine if their child is acting "normally." During the early years, a pendulum swing of behavior seems to shift about every six months.

Children typically emerge from the terrible twos into a time of contentment. Things that upset the two-year-old are taken in stride during this stage. The same child who had problems with his playmates now enjoys their company.

Unfortunately, this time of tranquillity is short-lived. Within six months the same child becomes insecure. Children at this age seem to be less confident in every area. During this stage, children may become clingy. As some children begin preschool, they are reluctant to part with their parents. The same child who six months before smiled and waved good-bye might now burst into tears or throw a temper tantrum when Mom or Dad prepare to leave. Three-year-olds don't know what they want, but they want it done their way, and they worry about everything.

That insecure little three-year-old turns into a bundle of energy, often aggressive energy, at four. Four-year-olds hit and kick and lash out. They sometimes seem almost bigger than life. Everything they do and say is extreme. Even parents who love to boast of their child's verbal prowess quickly grow tired of the inappropriate language adopted by most four-year-olds. This is the age when bathroom language really enters the vocabulary. And can they tell stories!

Exaggeration is developmentally appropriate for four-year-olds. Ask one to describe his summer vacation, or better yet Thanksgiving dinner.

"We had turkey, and roast beef, and hot dogs, and potato chips, and peanut butter sandwiches, and corn, and Jell-O, and ice pops, and my mother made stuffing with marshmallows!"

Four-year-olds seem to specialize in telling whoppers.

The pendulum swings back to the more peaceful side at five. Five is one of the ages behavioral specialist Arnold Gesell calls "a golden age." No wonder most kindergarten children are so lovable. Five-year-olds seem born to please. They are family centered, and they all believe their mothers are perfect—their kindergarten teachers, too. They obey the rules, they follow directions, and they work at being "good."

Most parents are a little shocked when their sweet, perfect five-year-old turns into a self-centered little tyrant. If you thought "no" was an overused word at two, wait until your child emerges from the five-year-old shell. From five and a half to six, children are in a stage of rebellion. If you want it, they don't. To make matters worse, they have enough energy to be defiant all day long. They are physically active, and they have one speed: fast. And then, just when you thought six was the most exasperating age possible, they turn inward and cause many parents to wonder what happened to that six-year-old ball of fire.

Seven is a more introspective time. Seven-year-olds are often loners. They would rather be off in a corner than in the middle of the action. The song lyric "Nobody loves me, everybody hates me, I think I'll go out and eat worms" could have been written by a seven-year-old. At this age, children can become absorbed in books, or television, or video games. They like to retreat, and they are very slow to respond. Most parents become fed up when they have to ask their seven-year-old to take out the trash at least nine times.

At eight, children are ready to leave their retreats and jump with both feet into new situations. They like to test new activities and new ideas. They are eager to develop their own opinions, and once developed, they hold fast to their new ideas. Their strong feelings can create judgmental attitudes, and they can sometimes be excessively critical of themselves and others. Despite this tendency toward criticism, eight-year-olds respect their parents' opinions. Approval is very important, and eight-year-olds strive to please their mothers and fathers.

Nine-year-olds seem to experience a pause in the swing of the pendulum. It is a time of fewer extremes in behavior. They don't rush into new situations, but they are perfectly happy to participate once they get there. Friendships become more important at this age, and parents are removed from their pedestals. It's not that nine-year-olds don't care what their parents think, it's just that they care more about what their friends think. They are more interested in what adults can do *for* them. Nine-year-olds like to fine-tune their skills. They may practice their baseball skills for hours. If your child enjoys playing a musical instrument, you won't have to nag to get her to practice. Scouts work diligently to earn merit badges. They need little encouragement from their parents to achieve, because they take pride in their accomplishments.

Children between seven and nine become interested in the opposite sex. They also like to talk about it! Sexual comments and questions about reproduction come up in conversation. Though this can be a little unnerving at first, it provides an ideal opportunity to get into discussions about sexuality.

When children turn ten, what you see is what you get. Most ten-year-olds have achieved a sense of balance in their behavior. This is the other "golden age." Ten-year-olds just like to be good. By this stage, they clearly know the difference between right and wrong, and most prefer to please. They enjoy a good joke, though sometimes their jokes are at someone else's expense. Unfortunately, this can sometimes be interpreted as cruelty. Most often they are just fun to be around.

For most children, the middle years are a time of flux. Rather than have behaviors swing from year to year, they seem to swing from day to day, sometimes minute to minute. A casual interest in the opposite sex begins to develop into a more "serious" interest in relationships. Adolescent children, beginning to break away from their parents, begin placing more importance on the reactions of their peers. On the downside, adolescents can be impulsive, emotional, careless, argumentative, fidgety, disruptive, loud, tearful, overly critical, and physical. These same children can also be caring, team oriented, funny, idealistic, charming, curious, and ethical.

Just as a child's behavior develops over time, moral comprehension also grows and develops as children become more capable of understanding another person's feelings. The more they can understand the "why" of behavioral expectations, the more they will be able to work toward meeting your goals. We want our children to behave not just because we told them so, though sometimes we are tempted to expect them to jump to our commands. Instead we want them to behave in appropriate ways because it is the right thing to do. (See more about moral development in chapter 8.)

It is helpful to know the stages of development most children go through when observing your child's behaviors. What is developmentally appropriate for a four-year-old may be cause for concern at eight. It is comforting to know that most of our children's upsetting behaviors reflect normal developmental stages and most will probably be outgrown. Though the knowledge is useful, "going through a stage" is never an acceptable excuse for unacceptable behavior. An occasional breach warrants your attention, but when unacceptable behavior becomes repetitive, you need to go on the attack. If your child's behavior is creating problems at home, in school, or in social relationships, it is time to develop a strategy specifically designed to modify behavior.

When a child's poor behavior cannot be explained or justified as a short-term stage, parents need to observe the child's behavior and think about the reasons behind the child's actions.

Melanie sat in her car outside her son's school. She planned to surprise him by giving him a ride home. Things had been a little rocky at home since she had separated from her husband. She thought a little extra time together might help Josh feel better.

She watched her nine-year-old leave the building, his head down. Josh walked over to a smaller student, grabbed his backpack, and threw it into the trash barrel. Then he laughed and ran away. Melanie couldn't believe her eyes. Josh had always been such a loving, cooperative child. She could hardly recognize the young boy she saw before her.

When children misbehave, most parents look inward. They try to imagine what they have done wrong to make their children behave so inappropriately. Most of the time they feel guilty. When we examine our lives and our situations, we can often determine the reasons behind our child's misbehavior. Most of us know when a conflict in our lives has spilled over onto our children. We can recognize those times when those conflicts are contributing to our child's behavior difficulties, and as much as possible we make adjustments in our lives to help our children through these difficult times.

Often, however, we are mystified by our children's poor behavior. We can't point a finger at an incident or a stage or an upset that has contributed to this acting out. What makes children misbehave?

According to child psychiatrist Rudolf Dreikurs, M.D., children misbehave for one of four reasons: to get attention, to gain power, to seek revenge, or to display their own inadequacy. Those of us with children can probably think of instances when our children's behavior has been driven by at least one of these factors.

In his book *Children: The Challenge*, Dr. Dreikurs presents guidelines for determining the cause of a problem behavior. When children use inappropriate behavior to get your attention, the problems usually arise when you are involved in an activity that does not include your child. Because your child feels he must be the center of your world, any activity that does not include him must be undermined.

Attention-Seeking Behaviors

Any parent who has tried unsuccessfully to have a telephone conversation while her child pulled on her leg and whined can recognize the call for attention. When your child whines, cries, pulls on your clothing, fights with his sibling, spills his milk, or finds some other way of pulling you away from your activity, and when the inappropriate behavior stops as soon as you become attentive, he is telling you he has an excessive need for attention.

If this is happening, examine the amount of time you devote to your child. If you believe your child gets an adequate amount of attention and he still exhibits these attention-seeking behaviors, several strategies can help change his disruptive habits. Withdrawal, time-out, logical consequences, rewards, and charting can all reduce attention-seeking behaviors. These specific methods are presented in the Discipline Strategies section of the next chapter.

Sometimes children's cries for attention are not excessive—sometimes they're crying out for what they need! With today's schedules and family situations, many children are not getting the kind of attention they deserve. We agree that quality of time counts, but time counts, too. It's tough to squeeze a lot of quality between work and dinner. We know parents who go from work to the health club before they pick up their children from day care. By the time they get home with their children, it's almost bedtime. Parents are exhausted; children are hungry and tired. There's barely time for a bedtime story after dinner.

Society makes significant demands on young parents today and sets increasingly high expectations. Both young men and young women are expected to seek high-income, high-prestige jobs that require long hours of work. In some cases, financial reality creates an environment where both parents feel they must work.

If children are receiving inadequate attention, an adjustment in material desires might be necessary to provide time for one parent to be home more often. Society tells us we can have it all. Well, maybe we can have it all, but we can't have it all at once! Parents need to set their priorities.

As one outspoken parent said, "It's not that parents don't have enough time to spend with their children, they just don't choose to spend their time with their kids."

If you are reading this book, you have made parenting a priority. In order to give your children the time they need, you may have to adjust your schedule. It may mean you have to give up some of the activities you enjoy, for now. Look at it this way: You get only one shot at this job. If your child's behavior indicates he may not be getting enough of your loving attention, make some changes and give him all you can.

Power Struggles

Most of us have at one time or another fallen into a power struggle with our children.

"You can't make me do that."

"Yes, I can."

"I won't do it."

"Yes, you will."

"No, I won't."

These are the battle cries of power struggles.

When children are hungry for a sense of power, they refuse to do what they are told. The more you challenge them to obey, the more they refuse. Dr. Dreikurs helps parents identify this type of behavior by examining the child's reaction. Children who are seeking power are not soothed by your attention because they are not misbehaving to get your attention, they are misbehaving simply to prove they can. This is the type of behavior that most often leaves parents feeling frustrated and angry. Unfortunately, it sometimes provokes parents to use physical force to "win" the battle. When children are involved in a power struggle, corporal punishment and force only make matters worse. When you overpower your child with physical force, she needs more than ever to find ways to put herself in control. If she can't be in control in her home, she may choose to overpower a weaker child at school or may use the overpowering strategy to win her battles with siblings.

This type of behavior usually makes parents very uncomfortable. Parents dealing with these issues told us they often feel pulled into struggles with their child. "It's as if a huge magnet is drawing me in, and I just can't stop myself," one explained.

As parents, when we have difficulty in this type of situation, we need to examine our behavior. If we challenge our children, make unreasonable demands, or take pleasure from the sense of power we get when we manipulate them, we then have to accept our level of responsibility in their behavior. When we behave this way, we teach our children to be unreasonably demanding, too. Parents who give angry commands, who are resentful when their child doesn't comply, or who feel their sense of self-worth is based on their child's obedience are setting themselves up for power struggles.

In this type of battle, the choice of words, the tone of voice, the use of humor, plus mutual respect can be instrumental in defusing the struggle for power. For some parents, this comes naturally. If you are having difficulties in this area, look for ways to modify *your* behavior first.

Feeling Unloved and Inadequate

Some children lash out. Dr. Dreikurs calls this type of behavior "revenge seeking." This is not necessarily "an eye for an eye," but children sometimes want to strike back. You may love your child with all your heart, but if he doesn't feel loved, it's not enough. Children who don't feel loved are hurt, and they want to inflict some of that pain on their parents.

As the behavior escalates, they begin to feel they don't deserve their parents' affection. They identify themselves as unlovable, and they go out of their way to make sure they exhibit all the characteristics that go along with that label. They say hurtful things, and sometimes they seem to be intentionally cruel. They select words to sting, and during these moments, children have an uncanny ability to find our vulnerable spots.

One mom we spoke to recalled some painful times when her sons were little. As a reading teacher, she took pride in her ability to help children who were having difficulty. When her children wanted to hurt her, they simply had to declare, "I hate reading. Reading is stupid!"

"They knew that would hurt me," she said.

Sometimes children who feel unloved strike out physically. They might pinch or kick or bite. They feel important when they can inflict pain. In these situations, parents are often tempted to strike back. If your child is acting out in this way, resist the temptation to respond with force. Instead, do all you can to make your child feel loved.

One of the most troubling causes of poor behavior comes when children just give up. They won't even try to improve. "I don't know" and "I don't care" are typical responses from children who feel inadequate.

Self-Esteem

Teachers, psychologists, parents, counselors, and school administrators agree that most behavior problems stem from low self-esteem. Low self-esteem affects all aspects of a child's behavior. It affects her emotions, her values, her goals, her need for attention and acceptance, her relationships with her friends and family, and her achievement in school. Parents of children with learning disabilities, and the teachers who are responsible for those children, recognize that difficulties with learning often contribute to low self-esteem.

Teachers recognize that students who feel good about themselves do better in school. Counselors know those who feel good about themselves get along better in society. School vice-principals, in their roles as disciplinarians, rarely have to intercede with children who feel good about themselves.

What creates this feeling of inadequacy within our children? Children have low self-esteem for a variety of reasons. Studies by Dr. Stanley Coppersmith of the University of California examine parental discipline strategies as one of the indicators of how our children view themselves. It is probably no surprise that his studies indicate children with high self-esteem have parents who are affectionate, loving, and accepting. What surprises many parents, however, is that these children also have parents who are less permissive than the parents of children who have low self-esteem. Parents who set clear and realistic expectations of their children and who hold their children accountable when behavior expectations are breached, have children who display a strong sense of self.

Parents who are often critical of their children and those who are unclear about their expectations and rules are more likely to have children with low self-esteem.

If parents do not feel good about themselves, it is difficult for them to instill a positive self-image in their children. Sometimes parents compare their children, and one of their children feels less capable. Sometimes children compare themselves unfavorably with higher-achieving sisters and brothers or classmates. These comparisons can do much to damage a child's self-image.

Physical punishment bruises not only the child's body but his ego as well. If your child does not feel valued and respected, if his opinions and decisions are not considered, his self-esteem will suffer.

When we discuss behavior issues, we are often confronted with the "chicken and the egg" controversy. Are the negative behaviors creating low self-esteem, or is a child's low sense of self causing him to behave in inappropriate ways? In either scenario, it is essential that parents take a role in assuring that their child will have a strong sense of self. We feel the development of self-esteem is a full-time job, and parents must do everything they can to help their child achieve the successes necessary for a feeling of competence.

A serious and honest look at how your child views herself and at your role in developing her self-image can go a long way in changing negative behavior patterns.

Children with self-esteem problems may sometimes be withdrawn and uncommunicative. They often express feelings of powerlessness. Such a child becomes the Little Engine That Can't. Instead of hearing the message *I think I can, I think I can,* that child's brain sends her a signal that says, *I know I can't, I know I can't.* Eventually, children with low self-esteem stop trying.

If your child refuses to try new things or is easily frustrated, or if he is overly sensitive, he may not feel good about himself. If your child has difficulty making friends or cannot maintain a relationship, or if your child always chooses to play alone, he may not feel confident enough to reach out to other children.

Children who need excessive reassurance, who question their abilities at all levels, who are clingy and dependent need a strong dose of confidence building.

Children with low self-esteem often have difficulty accepting responsibility. Many blame others for their failures or make up stories to compensate for their feelings of inadequacy. Children with low self-esteem often seek out companions who feel the same way. Together these groups of children engage in unacceptable behaviors ranging from bullying other children to gang-related activities. These feelings of inadequacy can lead children to lie, steal, cheat, fight, be argumentative, bully, blame, tease, and engage in activities guaranteed to hurt themselves or others.

One of the quickest ways to tackle behavior problems is to tackle issues of self-worth. Unfortunately, the strategies necessary to improve a child's self-esteem are not quick fixes. Children don't begin to feel inadequate overnight, and they won't begin to feel better about themselves overnight. Developing self-esteem takes time. For specific strategies designed to foster a strong sense of self-esteem, see the general parenting strategies included in chapter 8.

Fractured Families

The high divorce rate in today's society leaves many children deeply affected by this process, and they often exhibit inappropriate behaviors as their parents struggle through the pain of separation and upheaval. Very young children are known to regress in their development and worry about the welfare of the parent who is not at home. They sometimes have problems sleeping.

Children in elementary school may suffer in their academic performance. They may get in fights and throw temper tantrums.

Older children sometimes take sides. They may threaten to leave the custodial parent. They suffer many of the same emotions as the adults. They feel depressed, powerless, and grief-stricken. They are old enough to worry about money and about their own welfare. Many try to take on the adult role of nurturing their parents. Many—young boys especially—grow up too fast.

If your child is having difficulty at home, at school, or with his friends while you are struggling in an unhappy marital situation or going through a separation, your child is suffering, too. Unfortunately, many parents are unable to attend to their child's needs in the middle of their own emotional crisis. In most breakups, parents want to do what they can to spare their children pain. They just don't have the energy or the emotional strength to deal with another problem.

But there are ways to ease the pain for children. For starters, don't talk about your ex-spouse in a negative way. You may have angry feelings, but that person is still your child's parent. Attacks make the child feel divided. Your child is a part of both parents. When you attack your spouse, you attack a part of your child as well.

Don't ask your child to carry messages to your spouse or to relate tales about your spouse's activities or circumstances. Don't put your child in the middle. Your child needs to love both of his parents.

If your child is young, make sure she knows both parents have a comfortable place to live. Help assure her that you and your spouse are safe. Keep as many comforting routines as possible.

Most children feel some level of blame when their parents split up. Reassure your child at every opportunity that you love her, and the problems in the family are between you and your spouse. Love, affection, and attention go a long way in the middle of a family breakup.

Discipline strategies often unravel during a divorce. Children need secure, predictable, established behavior guidelines and expectations. Try to keep the rules the same in both houses! If you can't agree about anything else, agree to put your children's welfare first and agree on some basic discipline expectations. If you can't get your spouse to agree, hold firm on your rules in your house. Don't be intimidated by a "Well, Daddy lets me do that" or "Mommy says I can." Say instead, "This is our house, and in our house, you will follow the guidelines we establish."

Most families need the support of professional counselors as they negotiate the emotional battlefield of divorce. Help yourself and help your children: *Seek help.* Let your child's teacher or guidance counselor know there are problems at home. You may want to keep home matters at home, but school officials need to know when a crisis affects a student.

Take a deep breath, keep as much structure and routine as possible, and hold fast to your rules. The world is filled with children who survived their parents' divorce!

Pressure and Stress

Divorce is not the only source of stress for children. Children are expected to achieve in more areas now than ever before. We expect them to be good students, solid athletes, and competent musicians. We want them to be considerate and generous, interested in the community, popular with their peers, and respectful to adults. And that's just what *we* expect of them. Their coaches expect them to be there every afternoon. Their piano teacher assumes they will practice. Their teachers expect them to do their homework.

All of these expectations create an atmosphere of tension most of us never experienced as children. Many children are not able to deal with the push for excellence and fall victim to the stress.

Think about your behavior when you are under stress. Isn't that when you snap at your spouse, yell at your child, or get angry with your own parents? Our children will not always behave the way we would most like them to, especially when they are dealing with stressful situations. Some children regress at this time. This is when we should help them deal with the factors that are making them uncomfortable to begin with.

Marital strife, family illness, the death of a loved one, pressure to achieve in school or athletics, difficulties with friends—all these can make children tense. Perhaps we need to redefine with our children exactly what is important, and then adjust our expectations to a more realistic level. Set a routine that includes some quiet, uninterrupted time. Children, even preteens, love to be read to. Try to set aside enough time to read a picture book or a short story each day. If you can't squeeze in a story or a book, share the comic strips. Your child will benefit from your uninterrupted attention, and the two of you will experience one of nature's greatest stress reducers: laughter. We will talk often in this book about family meetings. These provide time for sharing strategies to help solve individual problems. When families band together, most stressful situations can be diminished.

Children, like adults, can experience a reduction in stress with exercise. A romp in the playground will help a young child unwind. If your child enjoys competitive sports, that's fine. A game of soccer will help keep her in shape, and it will help alleviate stress. If, however, your child doesn't like competition, introduce the benefits of running, or skipping rope, or riding a bike, or any other noncompetitive physical activity.

One of the simplest ways to reduce stress is to ask for cooperation rather than make demands. Instead of saying, "Jimmy, close the door," try saying, "Jimmy, I'm a little chilly, would you close the door, please." Rather than command, request. It works!

Self-Fulfilling Prophesies

Some children misbehave *because* they have been labeled "bad" or "disruptive" or "difficult." Often, parents themselves give children these labels. It is not unusual to hear a parent say something like, "My son Ross can fix anything—and it's a good thing, because my daughter Joni breaks everything."

Teachers are sometimes caught describing a child as a "troublemaker" or a "space shot" or a "handful." Children don't need to hear these self-descriptive terms too often before they come to believe them. Sometimes we create self-fulfilling prophesies by categorizing children in this way. If Joni's mother expects her to break things, she will. If Joni's teachers say she is a troublemaker, Joni reasons they must be right. Watch your words. They can be powerful.

Adolescence

As children grow toward adolescence, most feel a need to separate from their parents. They need to develop their own sense of identity, and often this process creates major conflicts at home. Parents are pleased to see their children grow and develop and often encourage them to take on more mature activities and attitudes. Unfortunately, most of us don't find it as easy to provide our children with the freedoms that necessarily come along with new responsibilities. In homes where curfews, dress, friends, grades, jobs, general neatness, attitudes, language, and/or activities become a cause for dispute, the issues probably stem from your child's need to separate from you.

Obviously, many of the strategies that work with young children no longer work with adolescents. Parents are no longer their major source of validation. Teenagers are much more likely to seek acceptance and attention from their friends. If that's so, what can parents do? Those families who provide their children with opportunities to express their feelings and beliefs but who stand firm in their value system and expectations have fewer problems, but some conflict just comes with the territory when you are parenting young adults. Sometimes you just have to wait.

When to Worry

When a young person's behavior changes suddenly, however, a warning light should go off. If your child suddenly chooses new friends, new clothes, or new negative attitudes and habits, or if your child begins to get into serious trouble in school, if his activities draw the attention of the police, or if he puts himself in dangerous situations, then the limits of normal adolescent behavior are being stretched. Under these circumstances, you need to question whether your child has become involved in the abuse of drugs and/or alcohol, or whether he has become involved in dangerous sexual experimentation. Because your child's life is in danger, this is not a time to be passive, trusting parents. Now you have to interfere and intervene. Talk to your child. Talk to your child's teachers, to the parents of his friends; talk to his brothers and sisters. Talk to anyone who can confirm or dispel your suspicions. If your suspicions are confirmed, seek professional help. It is very difficult to tackle this level of adolescent behavior alone. Seek out a professional counselor who specializes in adolescent behavior or one who specializes in drug and alcohol abuse if that is a factor.

It may be necessary to get help for yourself and your spouse before you can involve your child—but get help. If you suspect things are that out of control, they probably are. See chapter 7, "Getting Help."

With Friends Like These . . .

As children reach adolescence, the opinions of their peers usually override the beliefs of their parents. Your child's friends exert a powerful influence. When you like your child's friends and admire their values, you are in a comfortable position. But if you suspect your child's behavior has deteriorated as a result of the company she keeps, what can you do?

As with many things surrounding teenagers, it is a matter of degree. Why don't you like her friends? Are you judging them by the way they dress or the way they behave? Are you making a decision based on observation or suspicion? We all have the right to choose our own friends. By the time your child reaches her teenage years, she has that right, too.

You can model solid friendship skills by examining your own friendships. Do all your friends share your value system? Are they the kind of adults you would like your children to grow up to be? As you can see, the issue gets sticky. Are you willing to give up some of those friends who don't always make good decisions or act as good role models? As adults, we might admire some of the qualities of our friends and choose to ignore or simply tolerate others. We believe our friends have redeeming qualities that make up for their shortcomings. We usually don't give our children the same option.

This is the type of situation your child is in when he says, "But you really don't know him, Mom. Dad, I swear, he's really a good kid." Your child is probably right.

What about those occasions when your worst suspicions are confirmed? You know your child's friends are contributing to her poor behavior, poor performance in school, and poor attitude. You have seen some of the signs we mentioned earlier—your child is in trouble in school or in trouble with the police. You know your child's friends are using drugs and abusing alcohol. What then?

Your parental instinct will be to separate your child from that influence. When faced with a similar situation, one parent we talked to said she simply refused to act as any kind of intermediary between her child and those she considered a dangerous influence. "I wouldn't relay messages for those children. And I didn't hide it. I told them and I told my son I would not give phone messages. I let my son know I didn't like his friends, and I didn't approve of their activities. It was one of the most difficult periods in our relationship. At one point, I told him if he continued to get into trouble with those kids, he would have to live someplace else. The real test came when he continued with his dangerous behavior, and I told him to leave. He was gone for a week, and it was one of the most difficult weeks of my life."

Mary Eckman, one of the authors of *Why Kids Lie*, says parents can forbid their child to see friends and threaten punishment, but it may be more productive to tell your child exactly why you believe the friendship may be destructive. Most children, even adolescents, respond better to reason than to demands.

One of the most difficult things we have to accept when our children's behavior falls into this dangerous zone is that our child is also a poor influence on others. If "those awful children" are having a detrimental effect on our child, it is likely our child is contributing to their negative behavior as well.

Because the behavior of peers is such a powerful influence on adolescents, Paul Eckman advises parents to take extreme measures when they believe their child is engaging in antisocial and dangerous behavior. Because it is so difficult to separate a child from negative influences, he suggests sending the child to another school or to live with relatives. "Do anything to get your child out of that group," he says. "If that isn't possible, don't give up."

Of course, sometimes children will seek out negative influences anywhere they can find them. Their need to separate is so great that they will go to any extreme to violate your beliefs and values. This is a good time to seek counseling. Do all you can to persuade your child to see a counselor, too. Many counselors will meet with parents and then with the child and then again as a group. This helps everyone involved. As hard as it is to accept, it may not be possible to change your child's behavior, but you may be able to maintain your sanity.

Often, if we are able to survive these stressful years, our children change from those ugly caterpillars into beautiful butterflies. Ekman offers the following glimmer of hope: If we can hold out, our child's friends have less of a hold as children near the end of high school.

It is sometimes possible to help your child find new friends by insisting that, in addition to seeing the friends he finds so attractive, he become involved in an activity that promotes better behavior—a community-service group, for example. When surrounded by other young people involved in trying to make a positive change in the world, your child will be in a position to find friends who are a more positive influence.

Seek the support of other parents during your child's teen years. Stick together. If as a group you set guidelines for your children, they won't be able to play one set of parents against another.

Dr. Michael Buenaflor made the following observations in a recent *Newsweek* column:

The reason we have trouble controlling teenagers is they're too busy controlling us. They have more time and energy to organize a battle plan. They so often position themselves in win-win situations. On the other hand, we seem to "win" cooperation or peace only if we give in. However, that might be less the case if we start regularly comparing notes with other parents. That always makes teens nervous.

It might just allow us to "save ourselves."

Keep alert. If you suspect there are parents who do not support your behavioral guidelines, talk to them. Seek out their support. If they won't support the group, make that house off-limits to your children. It is unfortunate, but there are always a few parents who will condone drinking in their home or who will allow their children to have unsupervised parties. If these parents continue to be irresponsible, take your concerns to the police. It is illegal to serve alcohol to minors.

If you have friends with older children, listen to them. They may have sound advice. They survived. That alone should offer some comfort.

Our best advice is to remember you were a teenager once, too. You may have been less of a behavior problem than your child, or you may have been more troublesome to your parents. Ask them for their perception. You might be surprised at their response!

Unfortunately, many of today's behavior problems stem from poor parenting at home. Children are left alone too much. Their parents have few if any behavior expectations. There is little or no supervision. These parents create problems in their own homes, and those problems can create difficulties for the most diligent parent. They complicate your mission, but you can't let them get in the way.

Irresponsible parents, unruly friends, poor self-image, anger, a need for attention, a thirst for power—any number of forces can cause our children to misbehave. Sometimes we are lucky and can eliminate the cause. With that accomplished, the behavior problem disappears. Often, however, we need to examine our parenting skills and make some adjustments. As loving parents, we want to take an active role in helping our child overcome behavior problems. The next chapter presents strategies to help you with this task.

CHAPTER 3

Selecting a Discipline Strategy

In most families, some type of disciplinary strategy is already in place. It may not be a method you consciously developed but is instead a parenting style that has evolved into a successful way of encouraging good behavior in your children. In these situations, the discipline plan is almost instinctive. The family's behavioral and moral expectations are clear. Parents understand them, children understand them, and the family works cooperatively within the plan. If this is what is happening in your house, don't change a thing. As we say in New England, "If it ain't broke, don't fix it." Consistency in discipline is invaluable.

Still, despite our best parenting efforts, all children misbehave sometimes. An isolated incident of talking back, using bad language, hitting, and so on is no cause for alarm. These incidents require some response, but if all else is running smoothly, a systematic change is not required.

Changing Your Strategy

When, however, your child develops a behavior pattern that begins to interfere with your family relationships or relationships with his friends, or creates problems at school, you need a systematic approach to change the behavior. Under these circumstances, you are motivated to effect change. That is the first positive step, because you will need that motivation to follow through with your discipline strategy.

It's never easy to change. Experiencing how difficult it is for you to make a change in your discipline style will help you recognize how difficult it is for a child to change her own behavior pattern. Accept the fact that changes won't come overnight—for you or for your child. Give yourself time to strengthen your new skill, and don't punish yourself if you slip back to old patterns from time to time. Practice might not make perfect, but practice will always make it better.

Discipline Strategies

Discipline strategies are designed not to punish but to create a positive change. Used effectively, they will not only change your child's behavior but help you develop a new parenting skill. Because children and adults have individual personalities and temperaments, one discipline strategy does not fit all. What worked for your mother might not work for you. What is unsuccessful in your neighbor's house might be very effective in yours. What works for one child in your family might not work for another. Examine the discipline strategies presented. Find the techniques that best fit your family's style and your child's particular behavior problem. Once you choose a strategy, don't expect an immediate improvement. Change takes time. While you are working with a particular strategy, look for a positive trend, not necessarily a cure. Look for success in small steps, and be sure to acknowledge even the slightest improvement. If you don't see *any* improvement within two weeks, try another method.

Sometimes behavior will actually get worse when you begin using a new discipline strategy. If you usually drop what you are doing to respond to a child who is throwing a temper tantrum, ignoring that child might lead briefly to an escalation of the misbehavior. Because the child knows he got your attention by misbehaving, if you ignore him, he might think an exaggeration of that behavior *will* get you to notice. Try to think of this development as progress. Though the behavior has gotten worse, it will not remain so for long. Once your child recognizes you are committed to your new strategy, her behavior will begin to improve.

Whatever discipline strategy you choose, remember that discipline works best when it is consistent. Children need to know your expectations, and they need to know you will respond in a predictable way when your behavioral expectations are not met.

Strategies for effective discipline come in a variety of styles. Time-out, charting, logical consequences, rewards, negative consequences, ignoring, withdrawal, and the development of house rules are all strategies that can help modify behavior. Some children respond better to one method than another. Some parents might be more comfortable with one type of strategy than another. Reward-based methods may not be appropriate in your family. Logical consequences or ignoring won't work when the behavior is dangerous. Time-out is of limited benefit if it must punish you as well.

The discipline strategy should be selected to fit the behavior and your personality as well. Most strategies will work if you really want to change the situation. Whichever method you use, it will help to find a friend to talk to who can encourage you through any moments of self-doubt. At first it will be hard to be consistent and stick to your convictions.

One Thing at a Time

Often when a child's behavior has created a problem, families are addressing more than one issue.

Juan won't pick up his toys. He won't make his bed, either. He leaves his wet towels on the bathroom floor. His clothes are scattered across his room. He is turning into a slob. While none of his behaviors is life threatening, together they drive his mother crazy.

If Juan's parents try to tackle all these issues at once, they and Juan will be overwhelmed. Instead, they might try to make a change in one area. In their first step toward encouraging Juan to be a neater child, they could limit their attention to the wet towel problem. His parents might choose to use any of the strategies listed below, but they should not expect a complete change in Juan's behavior overnight. If he picks up his towel only once during the week, they must recognize that as an improvement and look for him to pick up the towels at least twice the following week. Eventually, with encouragement, Juan will modify his sloppy habits, and the family can then go on to the next issue.

Time-Out

Time-out has been effective for many families. For children in preschool and early elementary, it can be a successful strategy when used effectively. With time-out, children learn that misbehaving is no longer a way to get their most prized commodity: your attention.

Most of us can remember being sent to our rooms as children. It was a typical though not extremely effective method of discipline. When we were sent to our rooms, many of us cried for a few minutes and then picked up a favorite game or toy and found a way to have fun until our parents told us to come out. Your child's room is one of the least effective locations for time-out for a variety of reasons. As we did, children today have their favorite toys (in some cases their own computers and televisions) in their rooms. Sending them there is like sending them to the game room! Not only are bedrooms associated with fun, they are associated with comforting feelings as well. Most children associate their rooms with their security blankets, with bedtime stories, with their favorite toys, with warm, cozy feelings. This makes the bedroom an inappropriate place for time-out. A chair or a spot on the floor away from most household activity is a better choice. Remember, you want your child removed from any pleasurable activities in your home. You also want her away from the taunts of siblings. Get her away from the television, away from other children, and most important away from your attention. You may choose to stay in the same area and ignore your child, this being the only way you can be sure she stays quietly in the designated spot. But if you need time away from your child, don't hesitate to walk away from the room.

As a strategy, an effective time-out means more than merely removing a child from an enjoyable atmosphere. To be effective, time-out must be part of an ongoing plan. Children need to know when and why time-out will be implemented, and they need to know it will happen immediately every time they break a rule.

Time-out works best when it is part of an overall strategy for encouraging appropriate behavior. In order for time-out to be effective, time-in must be positive. Praise, rewards, enjoyable family time, and recognition for positive behaviors are all necessary components in making this strategy work. Reserve time-out for what you define as serious misbehavior. In your family, you might use time-out when your child hurts another child or you. If your child uses fighting, hitting, biting, scratching, kicking, or pinching to get her way, she needs time away from enjoyable diversions and time away from your positive attention.

In your home, you may decide that spitting, damaging possessions, yelling, name-calling, swearing, teasing, refusing to share, or tattling are creating major problems. Reserve time-out for those behaviors you find most offensive.

Once you have identified the difficult behaviors, make sure your child knows she will be isolated from pleasurable activity or attention for a given period of time if she displays the inappropriate social behaviors on your list. Use time-out only for those offenses. Don't use time-out for any behavior you have not designated in advance. Children need to know what to expect.

They also need to know what is expected of them. It may be necessary for you to model the behavior you expect during time-out. When you sit silently in a chair for as little as a full minute, you can get the point across.

Often time-out is ineffective because parents make it last too long. Most child psychologists recommend one to two minutes of time-out for each year of your child's age. Eight to fifteen minutes might be appropriate for an eight-year-old, but it is unreasonable for a four-year old. Some families find a kitchen timer helps children see the time pass, and it works to announce the end of time-out.

You may vary the time within the range according to the severity of the behavior, but once you have selected the behavior that will result in time-out, don't waver. If your child is to receive time-out for swearing, no provocation should be serious enough for you to overlook the incident.

But he swore at me first. . . . He made me do it. . . . I was so mad, I couldn't help it. . . . He deserved it. . . . I didn't mean it are all excuses children will use to justify their behavior. This is not a time for discussion. At another time, you might want to talk about more appropriate ways for your child to respond when frustrated, but not in the middle of your disciplinary plan.

When time-out is over, it's over. Don't rehash the incident that provoked time away from fun. Your child has completed his time-out successfully, and it is time to reestablish a positive relationship. Help your child get involved in another activity, and move on.

Traveling Time-Out

In order to be consistent, your child must know that the consequence of his poor behavior will be the same when the behavior occurs away from home. This presents a unique set of problems, as it is difficult to time-out a child in a car or in the supermarket. If you suspect you might find yourself in this situation, devise an alternate plan to meet possible situations. Remember, it is best to anticipate these unfortunate moments so that you will be prepared.

You may need to be creative to achieve this, but carry out your plan as soon as possible. This may mean immediately leaving where you are and returning home so that your child can be timed-out.

One parent says her family could never enjoy a restaurant meal. Whenever they went out to dinner with their children, their youngest child became disruptive. Together the parents agreed to tackle the problem head-on. For several months, they always went to a restaurant in separate cars. If their son misbehaved, one of them took him home for his time-out. At first their son didn't believe his parents would be willing to continue this method of discipline. He soon learned otherwise. His parents were consistent; and after several occasions when they had to take him home, he learned to behave himself in restaurants.

This strategy was effective because the parents planned ahead, they agreed on the strategy, they carried it out consistently, and they made their son responsible for his actions. These factors can make any discipline strategy most effective.

Still, it is not always practical to take our children home. When we are grocery shopping—or washing clothes at the Laundromat, or trying to shop for a gift—we don't always have enough time to go back and start the whole process over. Children usually take advantage of that. Don't let them get the upper hand. You can time-out your child in your car by telling her you will not recognize her or listen to her for a given period of time. You may seat your child in the car, close the door, and stand nearby until the time-out is over. Keep a magazine in your car to keep you pleasantly occupied during this period. You can go back to your activities following the time-out.

Sometimes children choose the times we feel most vulnerable to challenge our time-out philosophy. Have courage: Be consistent. You can devise a time-out spot at a friend's or relative's home if necessary. The location can vary; the predictability of the consequence cannot. Often these circumstances create the best learning situations. Your child will know you are serious about your time-out efforts when you remove her from pleasant activities even when she is away from home.

Time-Out for Objects

Sometimes it is more effective to give objects a time-out. When children continue to leave their clothes, their toys, their games in inappropriate places, they might have to lose possession of those items for a period of time. If, despite your requests, your child continues to leave his hockey stick in the middle of the family room, consider putting it away for a period of time—say, one day for the first occurrence. If he gets his stick back and leaves it in the family room again, take the stick away for three days. Eventually he will get the point. If he wants to play with his hockey stick, he will put it away when he is finished.

Time-Out for Mom and Dad

Parents can take a time-out, too. Withdrawing from the conflict works well with children who are determined to get your attention. If your child can capture you, even for a few minutes, by acting out, he will. Parents will recognize the following scenario.

Bob has been working at home for a year now. He doesn't miss the hour commute each day, he doesn't miss his necktie, and he enjoys the flexibility that working at home provides. What he doesn't like are the constant interruptions from his young children. Even though he spends a lot of time with his children at breakfast and in the early evening, they continually look for ways to get his attention while he is trying to work. Sometimes they whine; sometimes they fight; sometimes they spill their milk. When Bob loses his concentration, it costs him valuable time on his projects.

Bob's children will stop their attention-seeking behaviors and learn to leave him alone during work hours if he simply walks away from them and goes into another room each time they attempt to interrupt. Though this method creates an interruption in itself during the early stages, eventually the children learn their interruptions will not get them their father's attention.

As with all methods, it helps to be prepared. A stack of professional journals stored in the bedroom or the bathroom are ready to read whenever Bob has to leave his desk. This can accomplish two tasks: Bob gets his professional reading done, and he isn't bored during his time-out.

Time-out for parents is an excellent choice when tempers reach an unhealthy level. In stressful and frustrating situations, parents are sometimes tempted to say something hurtful, or even worse to strike out in anger. Walking away from the situation and allowing yourself time to cool off provides time to think more rationally. Your child won't get the unnecessary attention he was looking for, and you will get a little peace.

Parental time-out can be an effective lifelong learning strategy for children when it is used to combat abusive situations. If your child screams at you, threatens you, or strikes you, tell your child you will not stay put in an abusive situation. Then, walk away. As experts in child behavior Myrna Shur and Barbara Coloroso explain, when you walk away at these times, you send your child an important message: It is beneficial to remove yourself from abusive situations. With so many adults finding it difficult to disengage from dangerous situations, this is an excellent lesson for your child to carry into his teen years and beyond.

When You Can't Walk Away

Of course, we can't always walk away from our children when they act up. We can't leave a three-year-old to her own devices, and though we would sometimes like to, we can't walk away from our children when we are out in public. During these situations, take a mental time-out. If children are misbehaving in order to get our attention, we reward them if we respond to their behavior. Instead, try ignoring them. Imagine yourself in a stress-free environment—at the beach, reading in the library, having a quiet dinner with your spouse—and enjoy your "mental moment" there. I call this "Going to Aruba in my mind." It takes your focus away from your children. And children hate to be ignored. When we ignore them, they will do anything to get our attention . . . even behave!

If this is your plan, don't hesitate to use it in public. You might get critical stares from other shoppers if you ignore your child while she has a temper tantrum in the middle of the cookie aisle. Don't worry about it. This is your discipline strategy, and if it works for you, that's all that matters.

Rewards and Punishments

When we were children, rewards and punishments were typical strategies our parents used to get us to behave. When we misbehaved or refused to follow orders, some of us experienced spankings or other physical punishments. Others experienced a serious withdrawal of affection.

If we behaved ourselves, sometimes we got a reward. Maybe we got an ice cream cone if we made it through the grocery store without demanding candy. Some of us even got paid for good grades. Sometimes these strategies worked. Most of the time they didn't.

Corporal punishment continues to be a hot topic of debate. Though most psychologists, educators, and pediatricians believe that spanking should be avoided, a survey by Dr. Rebecca R. S. Socolar, clinical assistant professor of pediatrics at the University of North Carolina's School of Medicine, found that 42 percent of the mothers in her survey had spanked their children in the week before her survey.

Many parents admit they strike their children out of frustration, anger, or fear. Not many feel good about it. When we strike our children to get our way, we don't teach them anything more than that they will be hurt if they repeat the behavior. As Michael Schulman and Eva Mekler say in their book *Bringing Up a Moral Child*, "Spankings may be a quick way to 'teach a child a lesson,' but when adults displease us we don't teach them a lesson by hitting them. Your child deserves more respect also. There is nothing that a spanking accomplishes that won't be accomplished better, even if it takes a bit longer."

According to psychiatrist and child-guidance authority Dr. Rudolf Dreikurs, punishment is the least effective means of changing behavior. If smacking children worked, we would only have to spank them once, he says.

If we are to act as role models for our children, and if we don't want them to display violent behavior, it makes little sense for us to hit our children. In these situations, we teach our children that the mighty rule the weak. Children might obey when you are there to punish them, but this strategy has little long-term positive effect in changing behavior.

Shouting is also ineffective. Unless you raise your voice only on rare occasions, yelling at children has little impact. It embarrasses me to admit I yelled a lot when my children were little. With three children under four, I found myself shouting to get their attention, to stop them when they misbehaved, to keep them from running across the street, to get them to brush their teeth, to clean their plates. Seldom did they give me much notice when I yelled. As they got a little older, they even seemed to find it a challenge to see which behaviors would make me yell the loudest—and I don't think my children are unusual. Most children of parents who yell learn to ignore that loud, negative voice. After several screaming sessions, raising your voice has little or no impact.

Screaming in anger has no positive effect, and often the effects are negative and long term. Hurtful comments spewed in frustration stay with our children. When we call them names, they take it seriously. When we call our children jerks, or dummies, or brats, they believe they *are* jerks, or dummies, or brats! Though it's not always possible, try to keep your voice under control. Sometimes when our children frustrate us the most, we need to stop and count to ten, or twenty, or 100 if necessary. We need to give ourselves the luxury of time to cool off. Take that "mental moment." Sometimes just holding your tongue for those few minutes means the difference between saying something hurtful and saying something productive.

Punishing children does little to teach them how to behave, but rewards can create problems, too. When children receive rewards for good behavior, they sometimes try to up the ante. If you gave them an ice cream cone for behaving well on one visit, they might demand a sundae for their good behavior the next. It really is a form of bribery. Should we have to bribe our children to behave? Let's hope not.

Still, a rewards-and-punishment system can be used to motivate. We believe this system is most effective when the rewards are verbal or emotional and the child's punishments are natural consequences.

Natural and Logical Consequences

Sometimes rewards come quite naturally when children behave in an appropriate way. The child who remembers to put her laundry in the hamper has clean clothes to wear to school. When children put their homework in their notebooks before they go to bed, they have their work ready for class the following day. When they plan their clothing choices the night before, mornings are not as hectic. Sometimes it is difficult for children to see the positive effects of their change in behavior. Occasionally parents need to take advantage of those situations where a positive behavior change creates an opportunity for a positive consequence. Jarah's progress is an excellent example.

Eight-year-old Jarah loves waffles. Unfortunately, she usually took too long to dress for school each day to have time for a hot breakfast. She barely had time to swallow a glass of orange juice or grab a bagel before she ran out the door to catch the bus. With some planning the night before, Jarah began to get ready more quickly. Over time, she reduced the amount of time required to get ready for school so much that her mother had time to make her waffles, and she had time to eat them.

Jarah's mother added even more sweetener to the reward by acknowledging her improvement with her time and words as well.

"I love making waffles, and I love it when I have time to enjoy them with you."

Notice her recognition is very different from a nagging "I told you so" response. Jarah's mom recognized her improved behavior, but she didn't say, "I told you if you would get yourself together sooner you would have time for a decent breakfast."

Instead, she recognized Jarah's improvement by sharing breakfast with her. Jarah not only got to eat those syrup-filled waffles, she got some extra attention from her mother, too.

Reward your children with your recognition when they get it right.

When Janice's daughter Amanda makes it through the grocery store without taking things off the shelf and putting them in her cart, Janice makes sure she remembers to praise Amanda for her good behavior as they leave the store. When she tucks her into bed that evening, she adds that example of good behavior to the list of things Amanda did well that day, and she gives her daughter a hug and tells her she is proud of her.

When Mark puts his dishes in the sink instead of leaving them on the kitchen counter, his mother leaves a Post-it® note on his door with a smiley face drawn on it.

Jerry gives his children a thumbs-up sign when he sees them help their neighbor carry in his groceries.

None of these parents are effusive with their praise. They don't drool lavishly over their children every time they behave the way they should. They do, however, take time to encourage good behavior when they see it. These are all forms of positive reinforcement, and they serve as a form of reward for good behaviors.

Accepting Responsibility

When parents allow their children to accept responsibility for their behavior, negative consequences can be just as effective. Instead of spanking and screaming, let the child's "punishment" be one he brings upon himself.

Dr. Dreikurs spent forty years developing and practicing a behavioral strategy he called "natural and logical consequences." The strategy worked half a century ago, and it still works today.

Dr. Dreikurs suggested children should be held accountable for their behavior and that the best way to hold them accountable is to let them experience the consequences of poor decisions. Agreeing with Dr. Dreikurs, in his article "Teaching Responsibility: Developing Personal Accountability Through Natural and Logical Consequences," Dr. Don Dinkmeyer writes: "Just as adults who have experienced the inconvenience of running out of gas are most apt to fill their tanks when the marker nears empty, the child who has experienced hunger because he forgot his lunch is more likely to remember to take the lunch bag from the refrigerator before leaving for school."

Stephen McFadden, former vice-president of the Massachusetts School Counselors Association, agrees. According to McFadden, when parents make it their responsibility to control their child's behavior, they rob children of the opportunity to make their own decisions and to develop a sense of responsibility.

"The consequences method allows children to be responsible for their behavior by making decisions about what course of action is appropriate. This method permits children to learn from the natural or social order of events rather than forcing them to comply with the wishes of others," says McFadden.

Using logical consequences as a discipline technique requires more creativity and more patience on the part of the parent. Each situation is unique, and the consequence for a particular behavior must make sense within the framework of your family life. But through this approach, parents can avoid the power struggles and shouting matches often associated with discipline.

Tyler won't stop playing his video games. When his mother calls him to dinner, he continues to play until the game is finished. Sometimes this leaves the family waiting for up to half an hour for him to come to the table. The food gets cold. His older brother gets upset because he has plans after dinner. His mother is frustrated. His father starts threatening and yelling. Eventually, he comes to the table and eats.

When Tyler's parents adopt the natural and logical consequence method, the situation changes. They announce, "It is time for dinner, Tyler. If you want to eat, please join us now."

Tyler now has an option. He can continue to play his video game, but if he does, he will miss dinner. When dinner is ready, Tyler's family eats. If he is not there to join them, they remove his dishes from the table. He may not come to the table after the others have begun eating. They don't save Tyler leftovers. Snacks are not an option. If Tyler chooses to continue with his game, he doesn't eat. He has elected to play video games instead of eating dinner. The choice was his. So is the consequence. Most children love to eat. It shouldn't take too many missed meals for Tyler to learn from the experience and choose to join the family for dinner.

Much in this strategy has to do with word selection and tone. Notice Tyler's mother didn't shout, "Get in here and eat now, or I'm not giving you dinner!" She presented him with a choice, and she offered it in a normal tone of voice. There is no need to use sarcasm here either. Children get the message without it.

As with other methods of changing behavior, don't preach. It's so tempting to say, "I told you that if you didn't come for dinner you wouldn't be able to eat. Now you can starve, for all I care."

If Tyler comes to the table after the family starts eating, his parents simply state, "I'm sorry you chose not to eat with us tonight. I hope you will join us tomorrow." This method recognizes that missing a meal is unacceptable but the child's company is valued. It provides an opportunity to try again.

This particular strategy has worked in Cheryl's family since she was a little girl. Her grandmother was never concerned if one of the grandchildren didn't want to eat. Her favorite saying was, "If you don't eat, *you'll* be hungry." None of them left her table hungry a second time.

When we provide our children with choices, we give them the opportunity to make decisions. When they are allowed to both enjoy and suffer the consequences of their decisions, they become more competent decision makers.

The logical consequences approach is extremely effective for the forgetful child—the one who forgets his lunch, or his homework, or her money for the book fair, or her baseball glove, or his musical instrument.

Stop by any school office. The counter is lined with labeled items a parent has dropped off at school. Most of us are so tempted to bail our children out when they forget that we interrupt our own schedule to deliver a lunch or some other forgotten item. Once, OK. We all make mistakes.

As the parent of a middle schooler told us, "We are families and we help each other out in emergencies, but more than once is no longer an emergency."

When we continue to bail our children out, what does that teach them? It teaches them that someone will bring things to school when they forget them. Is that the message you want to send? Probably not. Let your child accept the consequences of a forgotten item several times, and you will find that his memory improves.

Creativity is key with this method of discipline. Sometimes it takes some time to think through a natural consequence to a child's behavior. If there is no natural consequence that would lead to a change in behavior, don't hesitate to design a logical consequence that works for you.

If your daughter continues to forget to feed the dog, maybe you will feed him her dinner. If your son "forgets" to empty the litter box, perhaps it will be necessary to put it in his room where he is less likely to forget. Children who don't brush their teeth don't eat sweets.

In dangerous situations, parents can't let natural consequences occur. In these situations, create a consequence that will allow the child a choice but does not threaten injury.

One mother shared her strategy. Despite continued warnings, Jenny, her six-year-old daughter, continued to run into the street without looking. Obviously she couldn't allow Jenny to run into the street, so she grabbed her arm and shouted at her. Jenny just didn't seem to appreciate the danger she was in. When this "grab and shout" method didn't work, her mother was tempted to resort to a spanking. Instead, she planned a logical and safe consequence for Jenny's action.

When Jenny darted toward the street, her mother said, "Children who run into the street are not ready to play outside. If you run into the street, you will have to stay inside." This strategy provided Jenny with an opportunity to learn from her mistakes.

If Jenny chose to run into the street, she was also electing to stay inside. After an afternoon inside, Jenny was given the opportunity to play outside again. When she still didn't heed her mother's warnings, her time inside was extended. She stayed inside for two afternoons before she played outside again. Jenny enjoyed playing outside, and she learned to make the correct choice. The consequence had much more impact than her mother's shouted warnings did.

One of the difficulties with implementing the logical choices method is letting go of the problem and allowing your child to make mistakes. We are quick to say, "We can learn from our mistakes," but most of us have a hard time letting our children make their own decisions when we know those decisions are less than ideal. Try not to overprotect your child. Unless it poses a danger, stand back and let your child experience the consequence of a poor decision. It is an effective way to learn.

As effective as this strategy is, however, other children benefit more from different methods.

Charting

Some children respond well when they can see a visual record of their success. The charts provide an effective documentation of success for parents, too. Sometimes behavior charts are part of a reward program that offers positive reinforcement as behavior improves. At other times, the process of adding a positive check mark or sticker is reward enough. Many school professionals use this charting method to help children overcome inappropriate behaviors.

There are two ways to chart behavior: to record the behaviors we want to eliminate, or to record appropriate behaviors as they increase.

With behaviors that you want to eliminate, you need to chart the incidence of the behavior. For example, if Susie's whining is driving you crazy, begin by counting the times that she whines at the dinner table. You don't need to eat with a pencil in your hand. You might want to buy an inexpensive grocery counter and keep it in your lap. You can push it each time she whines about something. When you start with a baseline, you then have a tangible goal.

After you establish a baseline, involve Susie in the project. Tell her that you have counted the number of times that she whined about something during dinner and you would like her to whine less. Make her aware of what you mean by whining . . . you might even demonstrate for her, taking care not to exaggerate, mock, or otherwise humiliate her. Sometimes children don't realize how they sound. Show Susie your whining count. If Susie whined fifteen times, her first goal would be to decrease the whining to ten times during the same time period. Don't try to do it all at once. Once she is able to control herself and has met that goal, try setting the goal at five, and so on.

Help Susie understand how she can change her behavior by providing her with alternative reactions. If she whines that she does not like a particular vegetable served at dinner, you can offer her a script for the same situation. Instead of "I don't like squash," suggest she make a polite request: "I wish you would make potatoes more often. I like them better than squash," for example.

At first you will need to provide an incentive for Susie to decrease her whining, which has met her needs in the past—she got your attention, and you probably made squash less often because you didn't want to listen to her whine. Now she will need to have other needs met if you want her to modify the behavior. She might be excused from her evening chores—clearing the table, for example—if she is able to meet her goal. Perhaps she will get to stay up a little longer, because you enjoy her company much more when she speaks in a more appropriate voice.

The following chart shows what Susie's progress might look like. Make the chart up so that it's easy for you to record information and for her to understand it. Between the two of you, decide whether the chart will be kept on display or someplace only the two of you will see it.

Day of week	No. of whines	Goal	Reward
Sunday	15	10	
Monday	12	10	
Tuesday	9	10	no dishes
Wednesday			
Thursday			
Friday			
Saturday			

Once Susie has reached the goal consistently over a period of time, change the goal. Charting a behavior helps eliminate nagging. You no longer have to ask your child to "stop doing that." Just keep counting. Often these behaviors are most annoying at particular times of the day. If you find your child's behaviors occur at more than one time during the day, target one situation. Tackle breakfast time, or after-school time, or bedtime. Don't try to deal with them all at once. Once your child has achieved success during one time of day, continue to use the chart for other times of the day.

Charting is most effective in reducing annoying habits. Behaviors that might respond include complaining, interrupting, tantrums, swearing, nail biting, thumb sucking, and so on.

It is much more difficult to chart an increase in positive behaviors because you cannot establish a baseline for a positive behavior that doesn't exist.

If your child never puts his toys away, it is hard to know where to start. You will need to involve your child in the project from the very beginning. Explain that you are tired of nagging and you don't want to do it anymore. Your child can help you by decreasing your need to nag. If he puts his toys away, you won't have to constantly remind him, but he will need reminders until it becomes a habit. Have him help you choose a reward for accepting the responsibility of putting away his toys. Remember our caution about rewards.

To help him get started, establish a place where his toys must go and a time by which they must be there. For example, if he is playing with his cars and trucks all day, he may not have to put them in their nighttime place each time he finishes playing with them, but he can get them out of the middle of the floor.

At the end of the day, they need to be somewhere in his space so that your living area is free from clutter. Keep his chart as close to his play area as possible so he can check off his task as he completes it.

Award a point each time he completes the task. Points can be accumulated until a set goal is reached. Once your child has reached the goal, he may receive a reward, perhaps a new privilege. More mature children who accept their responsibility might be allowed to stay up a little later at night or be allowed to visit Mom's or Dad's office for an afternoon. We don't encourage giving children material awards. As we mentioned earlier, a child with such incentives might begin by completing his task in order to gather enough points to buy a miniature car. During the next week, he may look for a larger reward—a remote-control motorcycle, perhaps. These things get out of hand very quickly. Try to reward your child with a new privilege or with your attention instead.

Your child's age should determine the number of points needed and how long it will take to reach the goal. Older children can wait longer for something they want than younger children. One clear indication that the goal is excessive is if it does not work as an incentive to increase appropriate behavior. Use the rewards that make you comfortable and make him work toward the goal. Here's a sample positive-behavior chart with a 10-point goal:

Puts toys away	Before dinner	Bedtime	No. of Points	Reward
Sunday	0	1	1	
Monday	1	1	2	
Tuesday	1	1	2	
Wednesday	1	1	2	
Thursday	1	0	1	
Friday	1	1	2	One game of Monopoly with Mom or Dad.

If your child has a difficult time getting into the habit and is having only limited success, you can build in nonverbal reminders to help him get started. If the chart is near his toys, you can point to the chart or establish a special signal, like a wink or a funny gesture.

One of the benefits of charting behaviors is that children learn delayed-gratification skills. Most children—young ones especially—have difficulty waiting. When they can watch their own progress and know they will receive something that is pleasurable at the end of their wait, they learn how to wait for things they want.

Behaviors that are appropriate for the increasing chart include keeping personal space tidy, helping with household chores, displaying good manners, brushing teeth and bathing, doing homework, following directions, exhibiting appropriate behavior at school, and sharing with siblings.

Established Rules

All discipline strategies are made easier with a clear list of house rules and a list of consequences for breaking the rules. This falls into the logical or natural consequence strategy of discipline. Professionals we spoke to found that a posting of expectations reduced the number of infractions.

In some families, children and adults create the list together. Children have a strong sense of fairness, and when they are involved in the development of the rules, they have a vested interest in seeing the rules obeyed. Sometimes, however, parents must accept the fact that they are the adults in the family, and they may establish a rule the children might not want to agree to. That's why they call us adults. A well-thought-out list of behavior expectations helps clarify the rules of the house for children, and it provides an established consequence for inappropriate behavior. Be sure to discuss the "whys" of the rules. Children, like adults, want to know why we feel these things are so important. In most circumstances, they accept the reasons behind our expectations. Children feel more secure when rules and expectations are clearly established. They need someone to take charge. Some children can keep a mental list of expected behaviors. Others benefit when these are written down and posted in the home. Either way, firm rules help parents and children.

Zack "forgot" to let his parents know he would be late coming home from school. He decided to go for a slice of pizza with his friends. Once they finished their pizza, they decided to stop by the library to visit their friends. By the time Zack got home from school, he was more than two hours late. His mother had already called the parents of most of his friends trying to track him down, and she was worried.

In Zack's house, the house rules state: "Zack, Katie, and Travis will call home if they are going to be more than half an hour late getting home from school. The consequence for breaking this rule will be a loss of after-school privileges for one week." For the next week, Zack will have to come directly home from school.

When Zack's mother realized he was safe and had been with friends for two hours, she didn't have to think about consequences. She was not tempted to respond in the anger of the moment with what might have been inappropriate speech or action. Though Zack might have been tempted to say, "I was only getting a pizza with friends," he knew better. He had helped develop the rules and consequences and knew well what the consequence of his behavior would be.

When families post house rules, the expectations are clear and the consequences are automatic. Don't hesitate to be firm. Some families find it most effective when they develop rules based on the specific behaviors that have been creating problems: coming home late from school, watching too much television, neglecting homework or household chores, and so on. Revise the list as necessary.

All discipline strategies should provide opportunities for children to improve. Once the discipline has been implemented, put the mistake behind you and allow your child to demonstrate she has learned from her poor choice.

With some new strategies for helping your children learn new behavior skills, you will be equipped to face all but the most serious behavior issues. With practice, these new strategies will become instinctive and will help you through the most trying situations. When your child does not respond to your best efforts, or when your child's behavior becomes dangerous, you may need to seek professional help. Sometimes parents find support when they get together with other parents or with counselors who specialize in helping families. In some situations, diagnostic testing can help determine the causes behind specific behaviors. Guidelines for seeking outside help are presented in chapter 7.

The consequences of children's inappropriate choices are often reflected in their relationships with their family, with their teachers, and with their friends. Each of these environments creates special difficulties and special opportunities for learning. We look at family life, school life, and social life in the next three chapters.

When you make the decision to try a new discipline strategy, give yourself a reward, too, when things go well. Record your progress in a journal and reread it when your confidence needs a boost. Parents who take charge can change their child's behavior, and parents who make a commitment to change are almost always successful.

CHAPTER 4

Family Life

Caleb got home from work at 8:15. His evening meeting had run longer than expected. He was tired. He hadn't had anything to eat since noon. He just wanted to sit down for a few minutes and discuss the events of the day with his wife. Before he had a chance to take off his coat, he heard his children fighting.

"Give me the remote control. You watched that last night. It's my turn tonight!" he heard his son yell.

"You creep, that program is junk! Why do we always have to watch what you want to watch? I hate those stupid football games," his daughter replied.

Before he or his wife could respond, the argument escalated into a screaming match. Kennethya and Leon struggled for possession of the remote control. Kennethya's hand slipped, and the remote flew across the room and crashed onto the glass-topped coffee table. The family heard the glass crack.

When a child's behavior creates problems at home, at school, or in social situations, the repercussions reach deep into the home and deep into a parent's emotions. Parenting has always been a difficult and emotional job, but parents are challenged more today than ever. There are more single-parent families, more working families, and more families struggling to raise children without the support of the extended families many of us grew up with as children. Families move more often today. Mothers or fathers sometimes work in locations away from their children. We just don't have the same support systems our parents had.

Because today's parent feels more pressure, guilt is a common emotion. If only they hadn't moved, or gone back to work. If only they had spent more time with their child or paid closer attention to his friends. If only they had more contact with their child's teacher, they think. Parents often feel responsible for the difficulties their children are having, and often they blame themselves for their children's behavior.

When we aren't blaming ourselves, we often blame others for our children's behavior. The child's teacher doesn't understand him. His soccer coach picks on him. His friends get him into trouble. Often we refuse to accept that our child's behavior may be the source of his difficulties.

We all want well-behaved children. When a child's behavior becomes a source of conflict in the family, it is difficult for some parents to accept. It is easier to believe a child is going through a stage, or having a personality conflict with a teacher, or is coerced by his friends.

The first thing to do to improve home life is to acknowledge that placing blame will do little to improve a behavior problem. Perhaps outside factors have contributed to a child's misbehavior, but if there is little you can do to address those factors, you need to address the behavior directly with one of the strategies we have discussed. You need to hold your child accountable for his behavior.

As school counselor Stephen McFadden advises, "Get over whose fault it is, and get in there and work it out."

Some parents just don't have enough experience with other children to make a valid judgment about their child's behavior. Those who don't see their children and the ways they behave in group situations have no basis for comparison when looking at their child's behavior. They might not recognize inappropriate behavior even when they see it.

Sometimes parents refuse to believe their child has a behavior problem. They think their child is simply going through a typical stage of development. "Oh, he's just being a boy" is a common expression. "He didn't mean to hurt anyone. It was an accident," some parents say.

But as an old saying has it, Where there's smoke, there's fire. If your child's playmates, your family, your friends, your child's coach, or your child's teacher believe there is a behavior problem, you probably need to look more objectively at your child.

Sometimes parents respond to their child's behavior in anger. Frustration mounts when children continue to act against their parents' wishes. When children continue to behave in an inappropriate way, their parents' emotions are overloaded. Shouting, demeaning, even physical confrontations often result. Anger is an understandable emotion. In families, it can be a dangerous one as well.

Negative responses rarely result in positive behavior changes. You can make a child fearful with physical punishments, but you won't change a behavior.

As we have mentioned before, many behavior problems come as a result of low self-esteem. Striking, screaming, and demeaning children will do nothing to change that. Remember, the parent is the primary role model. If you don't want your child to yell, hit, belittle, or demean, don't offer him a model of such behavior.

As suggested in the discipline strategies section, if you find yourself losing control, give yourself a time-out. Though it is easy to get swept up in emotional responses, walk away. Though many believe discipline is most effective when it is dispensed quickly, this is not the time to jump. Buy yourself some time to think.

Guilt, denial, and anger are common responses when dealing with a child whose behavior is out of control. Though they might be natural responses, they are ineffective ones. Guilt, anger, and denial do nothing to correct the problem that is creating turmoil in the home. Parents need to recognize that when a child's behavior has created an emotional nightmare at home, it is time to do something positive to change the situation.

Cooperative Commitment

When dealing with behavior problems, parents have to give themselves opportunities to discuss their emotions honestly. They need to talk over their ideas in a quiet, uninterrupted environment. They need time and space to evaluate their child's behavior and to decide how best to handle the situation.

In those families where two parents are involved in bringing up the children, mother and dad need to come to some consensus. Children are quick to play one parent against another when they know they don't agree. If you disagree with your spouse, don't do it in front of your child. While it is best when parents work together as a team, if you can't agree on a single strategy, it is better to let one parent handle the discipline situations. Children need a solid set of expectations if they are to develop good behavior skills. Most behavior problems can be handled at home if parents are willing to work together.

Christine Lenahan, the special-education director of a Massachusetts school system, told us that even in the most complicated situations, change is possible. "If parents recognize there is a problem and want to make a positive change, they will."

Emotional situations at home can contribute to marital stress. Couples need to recognize the impact of poor behavior in the home and set aside time to talk about issues. Their disappointment in their child's behavior, their frustration in trying to deal with the problem, and the constant bickering that sometimes accompanies parenting difficult children make home life unpleasant. It is tempting to drift apart during these emotional moments. If couples are able to create a safe harbor for each other in the middle of the turbulence, they may find that a unified and supportive effort can strengthen their relationship.

Single-Parent Situations

Those in single-parent households usually find the situation more difficult. Not only are they without a supportive spouse, they sometimes have a spouse in another home working against their discipline strategy. Divorced and separated parents should strive to develop a code of conduct they can both support. Unfortunately, disagreements over values may have been a contributing factor in the breakup of the marriage. If parents were unable to agree on a value system before a divorce, it is unlikely they will be able to work together after.

If you cannot work with your ex-spouse, set firm guidelines for your home and hold your child accountable to your expectations when she is with you. Many single parents find a support group helpful. More experienced single parents can offer suggestions for coping with behavior problems, and they can help validate your feelings and your personal code of behavior. Sometimes a relative or a close friend can help support the decisions you make about your child's behavior.

To help reduce the anger children exhibit when their parents divorce, try the strategies recommended in chapter 2.

Sibling Squabbles

Fights among siblings are one of the most common sources of family friction. Whether children, like Kennethya and Leon, fight for control of the television or for their family's attention, their arguing and bickering drive the most patient parents crazy.

The only way to avoid sibling rivalry is to raise an only child. All brothers and sisters fight. Whether they are nine months apart or nine years apart, children can get in each other's way.

Most parents believe their children should get along just because they were born into the same family. In fact, the children may be born into the same household, but they are not born into the same family. A first child had the exclusive attention of his parents for a period of time. The second child is born into a family that already has a child. A youngest child might be born to parents significantly older than those his oldest sibling had. While one child might have had an at-home mother during his early years, another child in the same family may have a mother who works outside the home. Parents grow and develop just as children grow and develop. Just because children are siblings doesn't mean they were born into the same situation.

Often we expect our children to enjoy the same activities that their siblings enjoy. In most families, however, children are very different. As Cheryl's boys were growing up, one brother enjoyed quiet, intellectual pursuits. The other was most content when he was involved in competitive sports. One didn't want to get up, and the other couldn't sit down.

My three children have common athletic interests. They all enjoy skiing or snowboarding. They all played soccer. Beyond that, their interests are very individual.

In a friend's family, Matt likes to play hockey. His brother hates ice rinks; they give him headaches. He would rather stay home and read a Tolkien fantasy. If their parents insisted the two do the same things, they would be looking for problems. These boys like each other, and they enjoy being together. They just don't enjoy being together at the hockey rink.

Another parent says she tries not to force her children to spend time at the same activity. One of her children enjoys horseback riding; the other doesn't. When she takes her older child riding, she leaves the younger one with a baby-sitter or with a friend.

When we try to force our children into activities their siblings enjoy, or activities we enjoy, they resent it. Think about your own brothers or sisters. How alike are you? Do you enjoy doing the same things? Let your children develop individual interests. They are bound to enjoy some of the same things. When you do things as a family, try to find a common ground.

When your children fight, try to avoid getting drawn into their battles. Usually the parent isn't around to see or hear exactly what provoked an argument. Once you take sides in one of these disputes, you're sure to make mistakes! It is better to say, "I wasn't here when this started. You think of ways to solve this problem." Then, remove yourself from the scene. Your children will probably be shocked the first time you walk away, but eventually they will learn they are not going to get your attention with their disputes.

The exception to this rule would come when arguments escalate to physical confrontations. "Fighting is normal, but hurting each other is not," explains another parent.

Though disputes between and among children are commonplace, parents can take an active role in helping reduce family violence. Parents need to step in and break up fights, but again try not to assess blame. Physical confrontations should require a time-out. If your children are young, time-out can take place in a neutral place away from each other. Try telling your older children they cannot talk to each other for at least half a day. Watch how eager they become to communicate! It will frustrate the daylights out of you, but they will be laughing with each other within minutes!

In addition to fighting for their parents' attention, children also fight about things. "It's mine!" is the battle cry. Though most children have learned to share by the time they are about five years old, that doesn't mean they will. We all have possessions we prize and are reluctant to share with others. If you think fights over possessions occur only with young children, listen to the screaming that can begin when a teenager checks her closet to find her favorite jacket missing!

Help young children appreciate the value of another person's treasure by asking them to consider how they would feel if someone took or damaged their prized possession. This empathetic approach helps children understand the value of private possessions and the importance of asking permission before taking something that doesn't belong to them.

Everyone needs a space. Some children have their own rooms. When each child has a room of his own, children should respect the other person's space. Let your children know a brother's or sister's room is off limits without an invitation in. Unless you have concerns about your child's health or well-being, you should respect your child's space, too.

When children share a room, the situation is more difficult. Still, each child should have a defined space within the room. If constant bickering occurs over space within the room, mark each child's space off with masking tape. Unless invited, siblings should stay out of their brother's or sister's portion of the room.

In any household with more than one child, some type of sibling battle is a daily occurrence. Though we need to accept that all brothers and sisters fight, we don't have to condone it. There are many things parents can do to help diminish their children's need to squabble.

Children in the same family fight with each other for several reasons. Sometimes they fight to solidify their place in the family. Oldest children can usually dominate by size alone. Youngest children can usually manipulate others by being the "cutest." Middle children usually develop extraordinary skills or habits for recognition.

Most often, children fight to gain attention or ownership, or to protect their territory. Because time is the most precious commodity in most homes today, sibling struggles are often motivated by a desire for more of the parent's time. When possible, set aside a special time for each of your children. One parent we know tries to spend at least a few hours with each of her children each week. She feels so strongly about sharing individual time with each of them that she hires a baby-sitter to care for one while she enjoys an activity with the other. She says the children look forward to this special time with her.

Not all families can afford a baby-sitter. In these situations, exchange child care with another parent in order to provide some one-on-one time with one of your children.

Dads should consider finding more time to look at their children as individuals. When I was a girl, my father often took my sister or me to watch the Colts play. Though neither of us has developed a lifelong interest in football, we both remember those Sundays with our father as special moments in our childhood. Perhaps your daughter would love to go to a baseball game or football game or hockey game with her dad. Maybe she would love it if her dad took her to the ballet or just out to lunch. Sons can enjoy special times with their mothers, too. Cheryl and I could get our boys to come with us anytime food was involved—out to breakfast, out to lunch. As long as a meal was involved, they couldn't resist.

In many families, children enjoy upsetting their brothers or sisters and intentionally provoke arguments. They sometimes continue the provocation until the confrontation escalates into something physical.

Sometimes they do it for attention, sometimes they do it for sport, sometimes they are upset about something else, or they are hungry or tired, and sometimes they do it for the same reasons people climb mountains—because their brother is there! In these cases, one child is usually the provocateur and the other is the victim. Help the victim in your house recognize the strategy. Her brother is trying to upset her. Help her see that if she refuses to rise to the bait and ignores his teasing, she wins.

Car Complaints

"He's touching me!" is a common complaint when families travel in the car. "She's looking at me," they whine. "He's bothering me!" they shout.

Nothing frustrates parents more than a group of fighting siblings. It is difficult to ignore the constant bickering and whining, crying, and complaining that is so common among children. But often, that is the best thing you could do. Though it isn't always possible, you can pull your car to the side of the road, get out, and close the door. Sometimes the shock value alone is enough to make children settle down.

If you are going to be in the car for any extended period of time, be sure your children have activities to help the time pass. If you can involve them in cooperative car games, so much the better.

Car battles are not easy to ignore, but as with all other confrontational situations, ask yourself, "Is this my problem, or is it their problem?" Though it is often difficult, one of the best ways for children to learn how to settle their disputes is for you to step back and let them. If you can ignore the noise, their bickering is not your problem. Tell them they have to settle their disputes on their own, and then let them.

If, after several weeks of this strategy, your children continue to come to you with their disputes, help them develop a list of appropriate responses and solutions to those problems that occur most often. These following examples might be helpful, but as always, have the children contribute ideas of their own regarding particular situations.

For example, when younger brother Paul takes older sibling's markers without asking, the older brother might learn to say:

"When Paul takes my markers, I will

a. try ignoring Paul because I know he is just doing it to make me angry."

b. tell Paul he can use my markers as soon as I am finished with them."

c. tell Paul that if he continues to use my markers, I will take his Legos."

In another situation, a sister might be responsible for destroying block structures. Your child might say:

"When Tammy destroys my structures, I will

a. ignore her."

b. tell her it hurts my feelings when she knocks down my structures."

c. choose to build structures when Tammy isn't around or when she is busy with something else."

Older children often have battles over clothes. A young woman battling this problem might come up with the following plan:

"When Barbara borrows my clothes without asking, I will

a. tell her I will take one item of her clothing for every item of mine she takes, and then do it."

b. offer to go shopping with her next time and help her find pants she likes as much as mine."

c. remind her that there are some items in my closet that are not to be shared."

These solutions work best if all children involved in the problems are also involved in creating the solutions. Children are imaginative and come up with creative solutions. Some of them are bound to make you laugh. If your children are not able to manage this solution development on their own, make it part of a family meeting.

Give Them What They Need: Your Time

Parents struggle to provide their children with all the material possessions they want. The "me" generation helped blur the distinction between want and need. Children *want* many things. They *need* time with their parents. As we mentioned earlier, attention-seeking behaviors are the most common cause of sibling disputes.

Too often the struggle to provide for our children leaves us with insufficient time to spend helping them develop. Few children suffer from a shortage of toys. Most suffer when attention and affection are in short supply.

Specialists tell us this lack of time together also means a lack of adult supervision. Children are left alone too often. When this happens, their primary role models are not their parents but characters on television adventure programs or sitcoms. It's hard to expect children to adopt our value system if we aren't around to share it with them.

When we do spend time with our children, we are often helping them with schoolwork or transporting them to sports or other enrichment activities. There just isn't enough time simply to enjoy each other's company. Few families have time to sit around a Monopoly board or to play Chutes and Ladders. Children no longer hear the classic fairy tales and fables read to them by their parents. Many young children have never heard the nursery rhymes. Picnics are almost unheard of.

Instead, if families do have any time to spend together, they spend it in front of the television. In many households, they can't even get together for that activity. Little Billy has a television in his room so he can watch his favorite programs while his parents watch theirs.

We need to spend more time together. If parents can schedule an early meeting with clients, they can schedule an extended breakfast time with their children. If they have time to work out, they can find time to play a game. As always, it's a matter of priorities.

If you need time to relax in front of the television, watch with your children. You might be surprised by the things they observe. As we mentioned later in the section on ethical development, when characters on television behave in ways that support your value system, talk about it. When they behave in ways that you find objectionable, talk about that, too.

Share a book together. When parents and children read the same book, they can discuss themes and values. Ask your local librarian for a recommendation, or join a parent/child book club.

Though it seems rigid, many families benefit from family meeting time—a period set aside to plan group activities, to discuss any problems the children are having, a time to share the good news in children's lives. Celebrate accomplishments during this family time and acknowledge children's strengths. When necessary, this is a good opportunity to reestablish guidelines and rules. Some families find it most productive to establish a set time for family meetings, say every Thursday at 7:30 P.M., for example. When the time is set aside, everyone knows not to schedule other activities during that time. Parents need to honor this time and make it a priority in their day, too.

Some families build in family time without necessarily making it a time for family meetings. Ruth and Richard, the parents of three young children, set aside every Friday to spend as a family. Though their schedules are busy and not everyone gets together every night, Friday night is special. Every member of the family recognizes it as their family time together. They share a meal, go to synagogue, and cherish each other's company for the night. Though many parents find weekend nights a time for socialization with their peers, Ruth and Richard are willing to sacrifice social engagements to provide more time for the family group.

When parents acknowledge the importance of family time, it sends a very clear message to their children. *You are important to us. We enjoy your company. We choose to be with you.* Children can only benefit from this kind of attention.

Don't Compare Children

Anyone who has raised more than one child knows that their personalities can vary. One child might be quiet and cooperative; another might be boisterous and argumentative. Still another in the same family might not care what anyone else does or says. We need to adjust our strategies to complement individual personalities and styles.

Sibling rivalry escalates when parents compare children. Sally might be great at math, but maybe her sister Elizabeth doesn't enjoy numbers. Maybe Lee learned to read before he went to school, but that doesn't mean sister Randi will be ready before kindergarten. Try to celebrate the differences and the accomplishments of each of your children. Comparing children is as pointless as comparing apples and oranges.

Though you may struggle to avoid comparisons, many children try to draw their parents into making judgments. "Which drawing do you like best, Mommy?" siblings might ask. How can you win in that situation? The only safe answer is, "I love both of these drawings, and I am going to put them both on the refrigerator."

Though many parents would never say something intentionally hurtful to their child, they sometimes get "caught" talking to friends or relatives about their children.

We have all overheard such conversations: "Andrew was always so good in math. Why can't Amy pass algebra?" When children hear those comments it does just as much damage as being told they're not as good as a sibling.

Though you may never compare your children, it is important to recognize that others do. One of my daughter's teachers said to her once, "Your brother never would have done that. Why can't you be more like him?"

Even in families where the parents struggle not to compare, children will inevitably compare themselves to their siblings. None of us is perfect, and we will not all excel at the same things. Think about how boring it would be if we were all great readers but none of us could write. What if all of us could crochet, but no one in our group could sing? Life would be dull and extremely limited. Try to enjoy your children's interests and individual accomplishments. Try to recognize, acknowledge, and praise your child's achievements. Don't hesitate to praise one child just because the other is nearby and listening. Positive comments don't hurt. Just be sure to praise your other child when he does something well, too.

It is a great temptation to label our children by their interests. I have heard parents say, "Phyllis is my student; Carmie is my athlete," or "Ronny is really a people person. My Jay is the loner." Before we know it, we have created self-fulfilling prophesies. Try to enjoy the individual qualities of each child, but try not to define them by their activities.

Children need to know there is someone at home who loves them for the person they are, not the person others expect them to be. You need to be that someone.

Being "Fair"

Siblings are quick to say, "That's not fair." Let's face it, life isn't fair. As we suggested in *Parenting a Child with a Learning Disability*, it is not even desirable to be fair. If one of your children needed shoes but his brother's shoes still fit, would you run out and buy shoes for both children? If one child needed a new coat and another needed gloves, would you buy them both gloves, just to be fair? Of course not. Maybe your youngest child needs more of your attention and flexibility during the week he starts school. Maybe your teenager needs your stability as she begins to try new things. Try to give children what they need when they need it. That is much more important than giving them what they say they want.

Things can never be equal. Don't even try. There will be days and times when one child needs more attention than another. There will be times when one child deserves a reward and another doesn't. A child's achievement can be diminished if everyone in the family is rewarded for it. Birthdays are for the birthday boy or girl, not for all the children in the family. Everyone has a birthday, but not on the same day. Stop trying to make everything even. You will drive yourself crazy. Give according to need and there will always be lots to go around. If your child knows he will get what he needs when he needs it, there will be less temptation to compare.

Children within the family should not be treated the same way. Older children should have more privileges, and they should have more responsibilities. Household chores should be divided according to age and ability. Keep reminding yourself that fair does not mean equal.

Tattletales

"Caitlin watched television while you weren't here."

"I'm telling Mom you didn't clean your room."

"If you give me that CD, I won't tell Dad you used his drill."

Tattling is common among siblings, and it creates real dilemmas for parents. Should they recognize the tattler for letting them know house rules were broken? Should they discipline a rule breaker when they know the tattler specifically tried to get his sister in trouble? It is a difficult issue. If you ignore misbehavior simply because one of your children discovered it rather than you, does that send the wrong message to your child?

Some specialists advocate ignoring any reports that do not involve harm. We don't necessarily agree. The best disciplinary strategies are consistent, but you have to judge each incident on an individual basis. If you know one of your children is looking for ways to get her brother or sister in trouble, you still need to discipline the rule breaker. You can, however, carry out the disciplinary consequences in a way the tattler will not witness nor enjoy. Be sure to let the tattler know you don't approve of tale telling.

In his book *Why Kids Lie*, Paul Ekman helps us clarify the occasions when tattling is undesirable: "Tattling is wrong when the child takes the initiative to inform, when the offense reported is minor and the motive appears to be spite."

One family we know has a policy that discourages tattling. Unless the incident involves harm, both the tattler and the rule breaker receive the same consequences. When used consistently, this type of plan discourages tattling for pleasure.

But what about those occasions when one of the children is involved in a dangerous activity? This can happen as children get older. As your children mature, help them understand the difference between tattling (informing about harmless activities or out of spite) and letting you know when a sibling is involved in a harmful activity. This issue can be discussed at a family meeting or during mealtime conversations, well before your children face such a dilemma.

When people live together, they don't always get along. This is true for adults, and it is true for children. It is unrealistic to expect your children to get along all the time. Work only on those situations that create chronic problems in your house.

Teach your children the value of compromise and of win-win situations. Psychologist Michael Schulman suggests sending your children into the "negotiating room" to work out difficult situations.

When both children refuse to compromise, a negotiator might help. Although as we mentioned before, parents should try to stay out of these issues, when children refuse to compromise or cooperate, the parent may have to step in. Some interference may be necessary. If the children are unwilling or unable to negotiate their own settlement, they will have to accept the arbitrator's decision. The mere threat of such a strategy is often enough to encourage children to work out their own solutions.

Chore Challenges

Household chores are another source of discontent for families. Children need to hear parents talk about household chores as an opportunity to learn to accept responsibility. The family is a microcommunity, and if children are to be part of it, they must accept their level of responsibility in helping that community run smoothly. As both parents work outside the home in more and more families, the need to pitch in is greater than ever. Many households are headed by an overtired single mother who simply cannot and should not be expected to do it all.

The earlier children begin helping with household tasks, the better. Even the youngest child can help. Three-year-olds can put the place mats and napkins on the table for dinner. Five-year-olds can feed the family pet. Make sure your child feels successful when he has completed the task.

All children should be held accountable for their own rooms. Moms and dads should not make their children's beds, or pick up their children's dirty clothes, or organize their desks. Beyond their personal space, children should be expected to contribute to their family community by taking on community tasks.

One of the easiest ways to get young children to help around the house is to give them the thing they like most: your time and attention. Rather than having your child pick up his toys while you do laundry, pick up the toys together.

"I'll help you pick up your toys. Then you can help me sort the laundry." Both tasks get done, and your child gets your positive attention along the way.

Of course, children also need to learn to take on some responsibilities on their own. Laundry is a family-produced chore. The scattering of toys is an individually produced mess. You may need to help your child get started; but then it is fair to expect her to complete the task on her own.

Some families distribute chores during family meetings. A list of jobs needing attention during the following week can be presented at that time. Depending on the ages of your children and the activities that need to be addressed, you can take several approaches to chore distribution. Easier tasks can be assigned to the younger children, more difficult tasks to the older children. If children are close in abilities and ages, chores may be distributed by lottery. All the jobs can be placed in a bowl, and children can select a task. In some families, a rotation system works best. That way, jobs are distributed equitably, and everyone has a turn at the least offensive and the most offensive tasks. Some families set aside a work time when all members are home. Together they spend an hour or two tackling the jobs that keep a family running smoothly.

Whatever your method, make sure your children understand they are doing these jobs because they are part of a community—not just because you say so. Be sure to notice when they do their jobs well and without prodding. Positive recognition goes a long way. Expect that tasks be completed.

Interruptions

Debbie bumped into an old friend at the grocery store. She hadn't had a chance to talk to her in several years and was eager to catch up. As she began to talk to her friend, her son Jeffrey began pulling on her jacket.

"Mom, Mom," he said.

Debbie said, "Just a minute, Jeffrey."

Jeffrey continued to pull on her jacket and interrupt her conversation.

"Shut up, Jeffrey," his mother snapped.

Because children love to have their parents' undivided attention, interruptions are a predictable occurrence. Whether you are talking on the phone, having coffee with a friend, trying to complete some work at home, or reading a book, it seems as if an invisible alarm goes off, alerting your children that you are interested in something else besides them.

All parents need some time for themselves, and it is understandable when they become annoyed at their children's interruptions. If you spend a reasonable amount of time with your children, it is reasonable for them to understand that you need some time for your own activities.

Some interruptions are inevitable, but with guidance, children can learn to give you the space you need.

Planned activities are the easiest to address. If you know a friend will be stopping by or you are expecting a phone call, you can prepare your child.

"Janet will be stopping by this afternoon. Your Legos are in your cubby. Why don't you plan to build a castle this afternoon?"

Your child will be less likely to feel ignored if he knows you thought about him when scheduling your visit.

Set up an "Interruption Box" filled with puzzles, crayons, toys, and so on that may be used only when you are on the phone or when you have an unexpected visitor. Explain to your child that these toys are reserved for those particular occasions.

Interruptions can also be reduced using a charting strategy or an ignoring strategy to help your child increase the amount of time he is able to wait. See more about these methods in the "Discipline Strategies" section in chapter 3.

Whining—A Winning Strategy

For many parents, the sound of a whining voice has much in common with the sound of fingernails running down a blackboard. It can make a parent's hair stand on end—provided they haven't lost their hair worrying about other issues. Sometimes, in desperation, parents will give in just to have the whining stop. Unfortunately, giving in is the surest way to have whining continue. If a child gets what he wants by whining, he isn't going to stop. It will become a strategy for your child every time he wants to do something or to have something. The best way to deal with it is to ignore it.

In some families, parents refuse to respond to children who whine. "If you can present that request in a different tone of voice, I will listen to you," they say.

One parent taped her child's voice to let her know what she sounded like when she whined. Now she reminds her daughter when her tone begins to enter that whining range, and her daughter can usually shift into a more appropriate tone.

Disrespectful Behavior

Wise guys. Back talkers. Smart alecks. These are the children who make parents wonder what they are doing wrong.

"I never would have talked to my parents that way," parents complain. "Who do they think they are talking to?" they ask. "They are so disrespectful."

What makes children think it is all right to talk back to their parents? Why does every direction turn into an argument?

Unfortunately, many of the television programs and movies that children watch present young people behaving in disrespectful ways. Children emulate the behavior and can't imagine why their parents then get so upset when they talk back or use bad language.

Parents need to let their children know that they will not tolerate disrespectful responses. Some parents look at this type of behavior as a tolerable form of rebellion. Renowned child psychologist Dr. Bruno Bettelheim disagrees. He says that when a parent permits a child to talk back, it is degrading to the parent, and as it degrades the parent, it undermines a child's sense of security.

Again, children usually use these behaviors to get attention. While you can't ignore their behavior, you can tell them you will not respond if they swear or talk back. Then you hold your breath and your temper long enough for them to get the message. It's easy to get pulled into a power struggle when children use this method of getting attention. Resist the temptation to respond in kind.

Homework Hassles

Homework is a constant source of conflict. Just the mention of the word is enough to send both parents and children into emotional turmoil.

As the amount of time parents can spend with their children is diminished, providing time for homework becomes more of a struggle. The children's lives are busy. After-school activities or day-care programs keep children busy until late in the afternoon. Many parents don't get home until that time or later. That doesn't leave much flexibility for scheduling homework.

When specific times are set aside for homework, however, it eliminates some of the arguing. Try to pick a time that is convenient for everyone. If you can't manage a perfect time, try to find one time that works best for your children. Though it might mean you miss watching the evening news, or that you have to give up some time having a discussion with your spouse, the consistency of having a set period for studies will ease some of the arguing, and as a result will reduce some of the family stress.

In some families, it is impossible to set aside the same time each day. Johnny might have Scouts on Tuesday nights. Sarah might have violin lessons on Wednesdays. In that case, try to see that each day has a set period set aside for schoolwork.

One of the best suggestions we heard while researching this book came from a school counselor's newsletter to parents. The counselor suggested parents call the time set aside for homework a "study period" or a "quiet time." All of us have heard our children say, "I don't have any homework tonight," or, "I finished my homework already." This new language eliminates those predictable excuses. Most students can use time each day to prepare for a long-term project, or to review a difficult subject, or to read a book.

Though you might not have to be directly involved with your children while they work on their lessons, it is best if you are accessible. If the children know you consider their school-work a priority, they will take it seriously, too.

Many schools now require students to keep assignment books. If your school doesn't, and you aren't sure what your child's assignments are, buy an assignment book. Have your child write each of his assignments in his book every day. When it is time for your child's study period, check his assignment book. If your child is inconsistent about recording his assignments, a phone call to the teacher would be appropriate. Most teachers are more than happy to help families construct a plan to foster good study habits. See more about working with your child's school in chapter 5.

As with discipline strategies, homework policies work best if they are started while your child is young. From your child's first day at school, you can schedule five- or ten-minute sessions. Good habits develop with practice.

Television Turmoil

As we mentioned earlier, television is a source of concern and discontent in many families. Siblings squabble over which programs to watch. Parents groan over program selections. Children watch television when they should be doing homework. Chores go on the back burner while television heroes burn down buildings.

Educators and psychologists have argued the effects of television for years. Whether you're a television advocate or critic, there is no question the tube eats away at time you could be spending with your children. American children spend twenty-two to twenty-eight hours each week watching television. Imagine the productive time a child could spend on another activity if we cut that time in half.

Violence on television has also come under attack from most parent and educational groups. Whether television violence produces violence in our children or desensitizes them is constantly debated. But I have yet to see anyone argue that watching violence is good for children.

Many educators believe television hinders our children's language expression, shortens their attention spans, diminishes their creativity, reduces social interaction, discourages physical fitness, and blurs the distinction between fantasy and reality. The list goes on and on.

Some families have elected to remove televisions from their homes. We support their decision, but neither Cheryl nor I were ready to go that far in our own homes. Find a time limit you feel comfortable with.

At twenty-eight hours each week, one of the biggest problems with television watching is the time it takes from other activities. Put a limit to how long your children can watch, and preview their program choices. Review the television programming guide each week and seek out those programs that have educational or social value. Sometimes even controversial programs can serve an educational goal if families watch them together and discuss the values presented.

When you limit the time children are allowed to watch and let them make program selections, children become discriminating viewers. When you discuss what you have seen, viewing becomes interactive. When you discuss the actions of the characters, your discussions can reinforce your family values.

Be firm. It isn't easy, but it is necessary. One parent said she hesitated to have cable installed. She waited until her youngest child was in high school before adding additional channels. Once the cable system was installed, she found her daughter watching MTV every day after school. She warned her daughter that if she found she was watching MTV instead of doing her schoolwork, she would have the cable channels disconnected.

Her daughter continued to watch MTV, and Mom canceled the cable service! You can, too. And when you do, be proactive. Tell the cable service why you are canceling. If the programs you find objectionable have sponsors, write to them as well.

Don't use television as a baby-sitter. You wouldn't hire a baby-sitter who advocated lewd behavior, extramarital affairs, violence, casual sex, or abusive relationships. When you leave your children unattended in front of the television, you give them an opportunity to look into a world that often promotes activities and values that you might find offensive. Many nursery schools now ban the physical, confrontational types of play associated with violence on television. They are trying to promote more creative alternatives for children.

Computer Chaos

Computers and the Internet have become strong educational tools in children's lives. However, computer games and access to the Internet also present many of the same negative factors we have discussed in the section about television. Children may spend far too much time playing computer games, and often these games promote violence. Excessive time spent communicating on-line is time spent away from physically interacting with friends; thus hindering the development of interpersonal skills our children need. Limit the amount of recreational time your child may spend on the computer each day.

Internet access gives children windows into many worlds we would rather they didn't see. Though Internet filters can screen some of the sites you might find objectionable, purveyors of pornography and hate are very sophisticated and often manage to find ways to confuse even the most advanced filters. If your family has a computer, place it in a location where you can view the activities your child is experiencing. Ask your Internet provider about options available for limiting your child's access, especially when you are not at home.

Day-Care Decisions

Children need supervision when their parents cannot be with them. Sometimes working parents have to find substitute daytime role models for their children. Finding adequate day care is a struggle for many working parents. When you try to find a caring situation in which your child's caretaker shares your views on bringing up children, the task is even more difficult.

In *The First Three Years of Life*, Burton White recommends having grandparents take care of the young children of working parents. Because grandparents usually have similar values, they provide the stability, moral guidance, and discipline consistency young children need.

If grandparents cannot care for the children, White recommends carefully selecting a day-care provider to work in your home. When selecting caretakers for our children, find someone who shares your values and your ideas about discipline. If you are unable to find someone to care for your child in your home, White suggests individual day care in the home of a trained day-care worker. When parents are unable to find an individual day-care situation, White next suggests family day care. In family care situations, the number of children in day care should not exceed three—two if the children are under eighteen months.

With careful screening, however, it is possible to find trained and caring workers in day-care centers who share your value system and your ideas about discipline. Be sure you find a provider you can communicate with. When issues of discipline arise, you will be much more comfortable sharing your thoughts and opinions.

Issues that create problems on the home front are usually predictable. Sibling rivalry, debates over television, homework, whining, and talking back are all issues families face. Finding adequate day care is a challenge for the most diligent parent. These problems are a normal part of family life, and most can be addressed with love, understanding, humor, and consistency. If you find your child's behavior leading to major confrontations, physical assaults, verbal abuse, marital problems, or undue emotional stress, don't hesitate to seek professional help.

Family life can be a source of frustration, but it is also a constant source of pride, joy, and emotional fulfillment. Our children are with us for such a short time. Before we know it, they are grown and gone. Those issues that seem to drive us crazy need to be addressed, and most behavior problems can be tackled at home when parents are committed to making an improvement. Take the time to make a positive change in your family, but also take the time to enjoy all the pleasurable moments that occur each day.

When things are under control at home, things generally go smoothly for our children at school as well. If, however, you are having problems at home, it is likely your child is misbehaving outside, too. Difficulties at school can be addressed when parents and school officials work together to help a child improve. If you have had a phone call from your child's teacher or from a school administrator, read on for guidance in helping your child resolve his school-related problems.

CHAPTER 5

Working with
the Schools

When Donna got a phone call from her son's teacher, she was surprised to hear that Justin was bullying one of his classmates. The teacher reported she had already tried separating the boys and had disciplined Justin by limiting his recess time. She said she had discussed his behavior with him on several occasions, and Justin continued to tease his classmate.

Anita was shocked when the vice-principal called. She told Anita her daughter had been caught smoking in the bathroom. The vice-principal reminded Anita that in-school suspension was the school penalty for smoking and advised her that her daughter would spend the next day doing her schoolwork in the vice-principal's office.

Marvin's evening reading was interrupted by a phone call from his son's teacher. Scott, he said, had failed his most recent test and had not turned in his homework assignments for two weeks.

These are all wake-up calls that parents need to respect. In most school systems, teachers and administrators try to solve school problems at school and call home only after their efforts have proved unsuccessful. The most frequent cause for phone calls to parents is student behavior.

Working with Teachers

Often, parents get defensive when they hear their child is behaving in a less than acceptable way. Sometimes teachers and administrators blame parents for the child's misbehavior before giving parents a chance to help solve the problem. When parents and school personnel join forces, most school-related behavior issues are quickly resolved.

When children are having difficulties in one area of their school life, problems often multiply. Seldom is there only one problem that needs to be addressed. When working with the schools, be sure to discuss all of the issues, but tackle only one problem at a time.

In many school systems, vice-principals handle discipline-related issues, and they tend to have lots of experience. The number of students sent to the principal's office probably hasn't increased over the past twenty years, but the issues administrators must tackle are more serious. Besides the misbehaviors that sent us to the office when we were children, there are the more serious issues of vandalism and violence.

Incidents of serious aggression are more common today. When we were children, young people sometimes "duked it out" in the school lot, but school officials no longer have the luxury of letting children solve problems this way. Because weapons are so easily accessible, and because so many children see problems handled in a violent way at home or in their neighborhoods, school administrators cannot let tempers get out of control. They need to deal firmly with conflicts between students as soon as they come to their attention.

School authorities recognize that most incidents of aggression are a serious problem, because students see them as a solution to their disputes.

There are more problems with verbal abuse today as well. Children seem to feel comfortable communicating with each other and school professionals using language that was unthinkable just a few years ago. Though some of these children learn this language in their homes, many of them hear it on television or at the movie theater.

Vice-principals today not only take on the responsibilities we would expect of school administrators, but they are often forced to take on parenting responsibilities as well.

Many parents have abdicated their parenting responsibilities, according to school officials—and those who haven't abdicated go in to bail their children out! No one wants to hold children accountable for their actions, and as a result many children are out of control. "Some parents are just afraid to stand up to their kids," one vice-principal says.

School administrators are put in an impossible position when parents turn their anger toward the schools and deny the problems their children are creating. Children who have difficulty controlling themselves often have parents who still haven't learned to control themselves. As role models for their children, those parents continue to send the wrong message.

What would school disciplinarians like from parents? They want parents to give their children the opportunity to deal with the consequences of their behavior. When children act out, they say don't excuse their behavior. Don't deny their behavior. Don't ridicule the people who are trying to help your child learn to control his inappropriate behavior.

If you get a phone call from your child's school, take a deep breath, count to ten, and listen. Sometimes we are so unnerved by school-related phone calls that we jump to our child's defense before allowing the teacher to explain what happened. First, establish why the teacher or administrator is calling. Is the call to let you know how they are handling a behavior problem at school? Are they calling to enlist your support in developing a strategy to address a school issue? Do they expect you to follow up the school discipline with an additional consequence at home, or do they feel the issue is being adequately addressed at school?

Sometimes parents feel guilty. They wish they had spent more time with their child. They know problems at home are affecting their child. Guilt sometimes develops into denial, and these denial blinders obscure what is actually happening.

Don't blame the school for your child's problems. Your child is in school only for six or seven hours a day. It is very rare for inappropriate behaviors to be related only to school. It is not rare, however, for parents to believe that their child's school problems are the school's fault. If you are getting phone calls about behavior problems year after year, it is probably not just a personality clash with the teacher, or the vice-principal, or the lunchroom monitor. Your child needs to accept the responsibility for his actions.

Teachers don't like phoning home. They would rather spend their afternoons giving students extra help, or developing lesson plans, or grading papers. Some afternoons they even enjoy having coffee with a friend. If you get a phone call, it is safe to assume your child's behavior has crossed the line. Give the teacher an opportunity to detail the incident that led to the phone call, and ask the teacher what he would like you to do.

Depending on the report, you might want to agree to a strategy while you are on the phone. Perhaps it would be better if you discussed the issue with your child before agreeing on a strategy. If that is the case, tell the teacher you will talk to your child, and set up a time to talk to the teacher again the following day.

Give your child an opportunity to present her side of the story. If her version of what happened is significantly different from the teacher's, don't automatically assume the teacher is at fault. Occasionally, a misunderstanding takes place, and parents need to be intermediaries. We need to be realistic, however, when we discuss a teacher's phone call with our children.

If your child knows she will be punished as a result of the phone call, she may be tempted to lie about it. According to Dr. Paul Ekman, a psychologist who has spent more than thirty years studying lying, the most common reason children lie is to avoid punishment. Most often, however, children will 'fess up and acknowledge they have a problem.

In a recent article in *Middle School Journal*, teacher Ted Levy reported that students usually acknowledge their difficulty in face-to-face conferences.

"If the student is present, I ask him how he is doing before giving my opinion. Nine times out of ten, I don't have to say very much more," writes Levy.

Until your child knows you have talked to her teacher, resist the temptation to set your child up. "So how was school today?" is really an unfair question if you know your child failed her history test or disrupted her math class.

Instead, explain to your child that you received a phone call from school, and tell her you would like to talk about it. Once you have both sides of the story, enlist your child's ideas to develop a strategy to solve the problem.

School Rules

If the phone call was precipitated by a rules infraction at school, and the school sets specific consequences for the infraction, don't get in the way. Support the school in its attempt to enforce their rules. When children make the decision to violate a school rule, they should be given the opportunity to accept the consequences of their behavior. Students who are allowed to suffer the consequences of their actions are rarely repeat offenders, a middle school principal has noted.

Not surprisingly, schools have more success in addressing behavior problems when rules and consequences are spelled out. In our school system, parents receive a list of school expectations at the beginning of each year. Parents review the list of behaviors and consequences with their children. The rules are posted in every classroom. When children choose to ignore or violate a rule, they and their parents know what is coming.

If you receive a phone call about your child's performance in school, you might want to arrange a joint meeting with the child and the teacher. Tell your child you would like to come up with a cooperative plan for success that you all—your child, yourself, and the teacher—can support. Together, develop a specific plan, ideally one that gives everyone a role in helping the child succeed. For example, your child will go two days each week for extra help; you will review his homework at night; his teacher will follow up with a progress report.

Learning Disabilities

Children with learning disabilities often have behavior problems at school. Children with attention-deficit/hyperactivity disorder (ADHD) have difficulty attending to tasks in the classroom, and their impulsiveness often gets them into trouble. See more about ADHD in chapter 7.

Children with reading, math, or language problems are also at risk. Because children with learning disabilities often suffer from low self-esteem, they sometimes act out in frustration and anger.

If your child has a learning disability, work closely with your school's special-education department to encourage academic success and to provide your child with opportunities to improve self-esteem.

Our book *Parenting a Child with a Learning Disability* offers specific strategies for helping children deal with their learning disabilities and the behavioral issues often associated with learning problems. The important thing to remember is that a learning disability is not a sentence of doom. It just means that you, your child, and your child's teachers will have to work harder and in a different way to ensure that your child learns what he needs to progress in school.

When teachers call to discuss your child's learning style, meet with them as soon as possible. When parents, teachers, and students work together, difficulties created by learning disabilities can be defined and addressed. As school specialists develop a new strategy for teaching, and as children learn new skills, behavior problems diminish.

Not all underachievers or students with behavior problems have learning disabilities. They may be frustrated by the instructor's teaching style. They may be having social problems in school that get in the way of learning. They may be expected to perform at a level that is too high or too low for their ability. There are many reasons for academic problems at school and it is important to determine the specific cause of your child's problem in order to decide, with the teacher, the best way to help him succeed.

Some children have problems in school with overachieving. If they are too concerned about performance, that can cause inappropriate behaviors also. A child who is too eager to please places a stress upon herself that can get in the way of her true potential. Teachers are alert to overachievers as well as underachievers and can be helpful in setting realistic goals for your child. Realistic goals can alleviate some of the self-induced stress children feel. Most parents I meet believe they are not pushing their child too hard, but there is a fine line in your child's mind between your being a pushy parent and a facilitator.

Bullying, oppositional behavior, excessive teasing, fighting, cheating, stealing, and lying cause problems at school. Most children have exhibited some of these behaviors at one time. They misbehave in order to be "one of the guys," to build themselves up in the eyes of their friends, and to avoid taking responsibility for their actions. When these behaviors occur too often, action is called for. You should be notified by the school if these behaviors continue, and you need to work hard to make sure that they are not habit forming.

If your perception of your child is very different from the school's perception of your child, it might help to have your child evaluated by the special-education department or the school psychologist. You and the teacher will get more information about how your child learns and why she behaves in a certain way. Specific psychological tests are described in chapter 7. In some states, emotional and behavioral problems entitle your child to special services.

Sharing Concerns

Though many families are unwilling to share their problems with school personnel, it is to your child's advantage to let them know when issues at home might influence your child's behavior or performance at school. When families are anticipating a move or discussing divorce, when there is serious illness or a death in the family, when family members are dealing with a drug or alcohol problem, children are affected.

As one school counselor we spoke to says, "Whatever is going on at home is played out at school. Parents don't want the school in their living room, but unless everyone works as a team, things don't get better."

It isn't always easy for parents to work with the school to solve these issues. Some parents themselves had difficulties in school when they were young and may react negatively as a result. Those who were often in trouble at school may tell teachers, "I behaved that way when I was a kid. It's no big deal." But if your child has willfully disobeyed school rules, it isn't OK. It *is* a big deal.

Also, when parents had difficulties at school themselves, they remember the unpleasant feelings they associate with school and don't want to relive them. If you spent a great deal of time in your own vice-principal's office, you are not going to enter it voluntarily to talk about your child. Try to put the past behind you and focus on your role in helping your child.

As one parent advises, "Approach this issue as you would any other job." Your job is to be the best parent possible. Your child's teacher is the professional who is helping you with this job. Forget what it was like when you were in school and forget your ego. When you walk into that classroom or office to discuss your child's behavior, you become two professionals working together to solve a common problem. You ask, "How can we work together to make the school year successful?" You and your child's teacher must work as equals for the good of your child.

When your child's behavior is causing problems at school, close interaction with school is a must. You might need to have monthly meetings to keep each other informed on the progress at home and at school toward a common goal. You will need to share strategies and progress. You might be surprised at the insight the teacher has into your child's problem.

Mary was amazed to discover that her son Brian's teacher had noticed how much of a loner he was. When Mary went in for a regular parent conference, his teacher asked if he had many friends outside school. Mary had been worried about the amount of time he spent alone. She had made suggestions and tried to involve him in group activities, but all of her efforts had backfired. The teacher noticed another child who appeared to be having similar problems and indicated she would try to involve them in working together in class. She suggested that their parents try to get them together after school. A close friendship developed between the two boys, and they were both able to gain the social confidence they needed to broaden their circle of friends. When teachers and parents communicate, many problems can be resolved.

If you are having trouble with your child at home, try using your child's teacher as an ally. If your child respects her teacher, the teacher can reinforce home rules as well as school rules. Many parents say, "Your teacher said . . ." in order to get the child to do homework.

Teachers can spot bad peer combinations that parents don't know about. They know how peer relationships can affect your child's behavior.

Lynn was concerned about a change in her daughter's behavior. Sheila began to skip school, and her grades were falling. Whenever Lynn tried to talk to Sheila about it, her daughter accused her of not trusting her and stormed out of the room. Lynn was afraid that Sheila was involved in drugs and worried that if she discussed it with the school, the police might get involved. Finally, the issue was brought to a head at report-card time, and Lynn could no longer avoid the problem. She made an appointment with the teacher with a sense of relief, and at the conference the teacher confided that Sheila's new "best friend" was involved with drugs, and that Sheila was imitating her friend's behaviors in order to cement the friendship. As far as the teacher knew, Sheila had not taken drugs, but she was probably very close. By working together, Lynn and the teacher were able to dissolve the friendship and point Sheila toward friends who were better influences.

Unfortunately, there are always individual cases where parents and teachers just can't communicate and work together. You may feel the teacher puts you on the defensive, or you may have corroboration that the teacher has a problem with your child and does not handle it in the most effective way. Teachers are not perfect—we are the first to admit that—and there can be roadblocks to communication. But remember, this is your child, and it is your responsibility to get through or around these roadblocks. You can do it directly by talking honestly with the teacher about your concerns and difficulties. Honesty is disarming. Most teachers will respond positively if you ask for their help.

When you are unhappy about a situation in your child's class, don't call the superintendent of schools. Though it might make you feel powerful to go "directly to the top," it is the slowest way to effect change. When you have an issue with a teacher, call the teacher. Under most circumstances, parents and teachers have a common goal, and issues can be quickly resolved. Treat your child's teachers with the same respect you would expect in return. Hateful notes, angry demands, and character attacks do little to foster a cooperative atmosphere. Set up a meeting with the teacher, and take your child with you to the meeting if you think it will help. You and your child will need to have a positive relationship with the teacher if your child is to feel good about the situation. Brainstorm about ways to help your child learn how to get along with the teacher, and be open to suggestions. If this doesn't work, you might suggest that someone else become involved.

If after talking to the teacher you still feel matters have not been addressed, ask for another opinion. Many schools have child study teams or teacher assistance teams. Ask that your child's problems be discussed, and attend the meeting yourself to present your views of your child.

Many schools today have school counselors. They often help bridge the gap between parents and teachers. Counselors have helped thousands of parents, children, and teachers solve difficult problems. Counselors can also be helpful when children are having difficulties with their peers. Whether a child is the bully or the object of the bully's anger, school counselors can help. Sometimes they orchestrate social situations in order to make children more comfortable interacting with other children their age. Some schools call them "friendship circles" or "social skills groups" or "self-esteem groups." They are all structured to help children make and keep friends.

Often a student's conversation with a school counselor helps a child through an emotional crisis. Children may talk to counselors about how they feel and the impact their feelings have on their behavior. Counselors can help children learn to manage their anger and find alternative ways to deal with difficulties.

School counselors often present programs covering difficult subjects like divorce, death, and personal safety. If your child is having difficulty dealing with these issues, find out if your school counselor covers these topics as part of a regular program. If not, the school counselor can meet with you to discuss your child's concerns and can then meet with your child directly.

In some communities, elementary and middle school counselors offer parenting workshops. Because what goes on at home has such a powerful influence on your child's behavior and performance at school, Stephen McFadden has developed the following guidelines for parents:

- Listen to your child and learn to treat him as an individual.
- Encourage your child to talk about activities.
- Praise your child and let her know you believe she can succeed.
- Acknowledge effort as well as success.
- Discipline lovingly and consistently.
- Show an interest in school.
- Visit your child's classroom and meet with teachers.
- Attend school activities.

- Give your child responsibilities.
- Don't compare your child with others.
- Go to the library with your child and play educational games.
- Be selective about TV programs.
- Start early with rules and consistency.
- Follow a daily schedule for homework.
- Consult, don't teach.
- Set a good example.

Of all the previous guidelines, one in particular has to do with a consistent source of conflict: homework. Parents want to believe their child when they're told, "I did it in school," or, "The teacher didn't give us any tonight." If there were no homework, life at home would certainly be easier. Unfortunately, your child would not receive the necessary practice she needs to fine-tune her academic skills, and you would not have a clear picture of what is going on in school.

Suffice it to say here, schoolwork should be a priority for your child. In order to improve your child's study habits, make learning a family priority. By doing this, you also show that school is important. Let your child know you support school rules, too; social harmony is important if your child is to learn to live in the world community.

If your best efforts and those of your child's teacher are not enough to solve the behavior problems that exist in school, it is time to consider outside intervention. If your child continues to display inappropriate behaviors, he may be asking for help beyond what you and his teachers are able to provide. Counseling may be in order. Chapter 7 reviews more serious behavioral problems that require professional help. Use the resources available to achieve the desired result: a happy child who is able to learn and get along in the school community.

School Phobia

Excessive absences, tardiness, and school phobia (an intense fear of going to school) may be a result of difficulties at home. When these behaviors occur, your child's schoolwork will suffer. These behaviors are a symptom of a much greater problem that should be addressed before it becomes worse.

A child who fights with parents each day before going to school arrives at school in a bad mood and leaves a very discouraged parent at home. Both school life and home life suffer. If your child is constantly in the nurse's office asking to go home, or if he has a tummy ache or a headache each morning, he is telling you something is not right.

School nurses can be another resource for parents. If you suspect your child's physical ailments may be school related, talk to the school nurse. Nurses see more children in a day than parents would ever imagine. They are excellent evaluators of children's levels of stress and their emotional well-being.

You also need to look at what is happening at school and at home for a clue to this need to be home.

When parents work closely with the school, it is usually easy to tackle the "problems" that are causing a child's anxiety. Sometimes children perceive incidents at school as much more serious than they are. Maybe a child is upset because her best friend is having lunch with someone else. Maybe a teacher's style is loud and threatening to a sensitive child. Maybe a child was scolded in school for running in the halls. Children don't always see these incidents as minor.

Try to listen carefully when your child talks about school. When she says, "I hate school," you may have to do more than ask why. When you respond to your child with expressions like "I can see you are unhappy" or "I understand you are discouraged" or "I can see you are feeling left out," you open the conversational door. When you acknowledge your child's feelings and emotions, you let her know it is OK to talk about her problem. Share what you learn from your child with her teacher. When teachers know a child is fearful or worried about a school situation, they can provide the extra attention necessary to help that child through the difficult moments. Once these issues are resolved, children are happier about going to school. The birth of a new sibling or a family adoption can sometimes create a problem with school attendance. Young children can feel their positions usurped by the new arrival, and they feel threatened. They want to be at home, too, so their parents won't forget about them.

In some situations, however, serious issues at home create significant emotional turmoil for a child. In order to feel secure, children need control in their lives. When that control begins to fail, children try to fill the void. They make themselves responsible for keeping things under control at home. Children of alcoholics or drug abusers know their parents are unable to hold things together at home. If they have younger brothers or sisters at home, children want to be there to care for them. Sometimes they want to be there to care for the parents!

Children who have experienced abandonment or homelessness are frightened they will lose a parent or a place to live in again. They feel more secure when they are at home with their parents.

Whether the problem is minor or major, children need to be in school. Don't give in to the temptation to keep your child home. That rewards the behaviors—crying, tantrums, physical symptoms—students exhibit when they are afraid of school. If going to school continues to be a problem for your child, consult your pediatrician, the school counselor, or a psychologist.

School phobia can often be avoided with adequate preparation. Sometimes a child's anxiety is related more to anticipation than to actual circumstances. If your child is transferring schools, or attending a new school for the first time, be sure to visit the school before the first day. Check out the school office, find the bathrooms, go to the cafeteria, and introduce your child to his teacher and to several other adults in the building.

Give your child realistic expectations about school. There will be playtime and work time. When children are adequately prepared, new school situations usually don't create problems.

Most school issues can be resolved quickly when parents work closely with school officials. Parents and teachers share a common goal: the nurturing and instruction of children. Look to your school as a source of support, and support your child's teachers and school administrators when they call on you. For more information about school phobia, see the "Anxiety Disorders" section of chapter 7.

CHAPTER 6

Making and Keeping Friends

Clarise worried because her daughter Paula hadn't made any friends at her new school. Clarise knew it was difficult for Paula to share her toys, and she knew Paula sometimes hit other children. Though the kindergarten teacher had mentioned Paula's lack of self-control, Clarise was convinced it was simply a stage her daughter would outgrow. When Paula was the only little girl who did not receive an invitation to a classmate's birthday party, Clarise had to accept the fact that the children in her class were ostracizing Paula.

Nothing breaks a parent's heart faster than seeing a child left out. We all want our children to have friends they can play with, friends they can talk to, friends they can just be with. We want them to be invited to birthday parties, and to pickup baseball games. We want to see them involved in athletic or social groups with children their own age. We want them to be socially successful.

When children have trouble making or keeping friends, behavior problems are often at the heart of the problem. Shy children, mean children, children who are aggressive or are bullies, children who are victims, children who tattle, bossy children, children who name-call, children who won't share, those who refuse to take turns or wait their turn, children who are poor sports, children who boast and brag, and children who tease often have trouble making friends.

If your child is having difficulty making friends, try to observe your child objectively. If you have a friend who will be honest with you, ask for her opinion—and don't get angry with her when she tells you the truth.

All children display some antisocial behaviors during their stages of growing up. But when these behaviors become routine for your child, they get in the way. You need to work on changing your child's behavior before you can expect his social life to change. Parents cannot orchestrate friendships if their children behave in a way that other children find offensive.

We've all seen parents who go out of their way to surround their children with playmates—the parent who will take a dozen children to the zoo in the hopes of finding one friend for her child, the father who will rent ice space and invite a team of hockey enthusiasts in the hopes of elevating his son's position in the social group. These attempts are almost always unsuccessful. You can't buy friends.

What you can do is help your child improve his behavior. Almost all antisocial behaviors are the result of low self-esteem. Children are hurtful toward other children in order to make themselves feel more important. They are also mean because it is expedient. Aggressive behaviors call for your immediate attention. If these behaviors are ignored, they quickly escalate into major problems.

If your child is acting out in a way that prevents him from making friends, try to elevate his self-esteem. Strategies for developing self-esteem are outlined in chapter 8.

A child who has difficulty making friends now won't have any friends by the time she reaches adolescence if the behavior patterns are not short-circuited. Children who bully to get their way need to develop the ability to give and take before they can attract friends.

Sometimes children are aggressive because they are upset about other areas of their life. If there is stress at home, your child might act it out in social situations. If you believe stress might be leading to your child's aggressive behavior, do what you can to make your child feel more secure.

If your child admits she is having trouble making or keeping friends, don't deny the problem. If she says, "Nobody likes me," use it as an opportunity to talk. If you have seen your child behave in an antisocial way, talk about the behavior. Point out that children feel threatened when they are bullied, or that children don't like to be called names, and so on. Help your child see that his behavior is getting in the way. Ask your child what he would expect from a friend. How would he expect a friend to behave toward him? It might even be helpful to role-play social situations in order to help your child find alternative behaviors.

Sometimes children don't recognize their behaviors as troublesome. If we can point to other examples of poor behavior, sometimes children can begin to recognize the behavior problem in themselves. Characters from literature, television, or films can often provide an example of both inappropriate behavior and more appropriate behaviors. Beauty's love for the Beast, Snow White's friendship with the seven dwarfs, the support Piglet and Winnie give each other are excellent examples of caring and friendship. Rather than point to other children as examples of appropriate behavior (children often resent this), point to fictional characters and situations.

Catch your child in the act when he displays appropriate behaviors. If he waits in line patiently at the ice cream truck, or shares his toys, or says something nice to a peer, be sure to notice. When we credit them for their good behavior, we reinforce those behaviors.

Unfortunately, we sometimes model inappropriate behavior ourselves. If you or your spouse teases in humor, your child may not have refined his teasing talents to the point where children find them funny. Give up teasing for a while.

If we bully our children into following our orders, we shouldn't be surprised if they bully as well. When we strike our children, we communicate to them that hitting other people is acceptable. When we call names and shout at each other, we are poor role models.

If your child is not exhibiting antisocial behaviors but is still having trouble making friends, take an objective look at your child's personality. Is he shy? Is he afraid of new situations? Again, we can help by fostering self-esteem.

We can also help our children by providing them with scripts of what they can say in social situations. If children normally get a "no" response to the "Do you want to play?" question, you can have them experiment with a change in language.

"Can we play later?" usually gets a positive response. Help your child be prepared for a "yes" answer. The child can suggest a time to play.

Remind your child to look at the person he is talking to. Eye contact is important. If your child whispers, help him practice using a bigger voice.

Because shy children seldom take a leadership role, provide opportunities for your child to play with younger children. The age difference will help your child be more confident and will give him practice in taking control of social situations.

This is an occasion where television can actually help. Watch with your child and discuss the ways the television characters handle social situations—the way Ernie and Bert talk to each other, for example. Practice social interactions with puppets. Take turns being the person who initiates the conversation. As with most skills, practice helps.

Occasionally, shyness is due to stress in a child's life. If you can reduce the stress, sometimes children become more involved in social activities.

Still, some children are naturally less outgoing and social than others. Perhaps your child won't be a social butterfly or take the lead in the school play. Maybe he will write for the school newspaper or be the star of the chess team.

When simple shyness develops into withdrawal, parents need to be concerned. A child who stays in his room all day, who doesn't return phone calls, who refuses invitations, or who appears to be depressed is calling for help. Contact your pediatrician or a mental health professional if your child's behavior is extreme. For more information about depression, see chapter 7.

Though it isn't discussed very often, personal hygiene can be a factor when children are having trouble in social situations. Children who refuse to bathe or brush their teeth or wash their hair are not welcome in most social circles. If these conditions prevail, help your child see the logical consequence of his poor personal habits.

Don't label children. Referring to them as shy or aggressive or rowdy will only invite them to rise to our expectations. Don't tease them, either. Teasing can be hurtful and does little to help children who are less than confident.

Invisible Handicaps

Sometimes children have invisible social handicaps that get in the way. Children with language difficulties often have trouble. Speech impediments make it difficult to communicate. Children with receptive language disorders have trouble interpreting what other children say. Sometimes they even have trouble remembering what was said.

If adults refer to your child as "tactless," "rude," or "socially immature," or if you hear other children call her "stupid" or "dumb," your child might have a receptive language problem. If you suspect your child is having trouble understanding social language, seek help from your school professionals. Educators are specially trained to help your child develop in this area.

Some children are unable to understand the body language that is so important when young people communicate. Children with normal skills in this area know when to approach another child and when not to. They know a child who has his arms folded across his chest and is wearing a scowl on his face is not waiting to greet a new friend.

Children with body language disabilities can't see that physical message. Children jostle with each other as part of their playtime. Children with poor body language skills don't know the difference between jostling and punching. The distinction is lost on them, and so the ability to foster a friendship is lost, too.

We can help children who have difficulties with nonverbal communication. Help your child study your facial expressions as you make happy faces and sad faces and angry faces. Talk to him about the differences in the expressions. Turn the sound off on the television. Watch the expressions of the characters. Describe the expressive body language you are watching to your child.

Sometimes children with this disorder have trouble adjusting the tone or the volume of their voice.

Recently, I helped a young boy in our school "hear" the difference between the way he "asked" for help and the way I like to hear students request it. When I spoke back to him in the same demeaning tone he used to speak to me, he looked at me in surprise. "Do I really sound like that?" he asked.

Since then we have practiced. Now he usually asks for help in an appropriate tone of voice.

Children with these language disorders need help. You can help your child at home, and when school professionals know about the difficulty, they can support your child's progress at school as well.

Attention deficit hyperactivity disorder can also complicate social situations. Where children with ADHD often have difficulty attending to tasks in the classroom, their problems can also make it hard for them to make friends. Their impulsive behavior can get them into verbal and physical confrontations. They don't always have the control necessary to think before they speak or act. Sometimes their constant motion makes other children nervous. If you suspect your child has ADHD, consult your pediatrician. If your child is diagnosed with ADHD, specific strategies can be used to help your child at home.

To facilitate social situations, invite only one child to play at a time. Hyperactive children need more structure in their playtime. Keep activities short, and shift games often. You might have him play on the swings with a friend for ten minutes and then give them a ball to play with. After a short period of time, interrupt their play for some snacks.

If your child has been diagnosed with ADHD, your school's special education staff can be an excellent source of support and advice. See chapter 7 for more information on ADHD.

Differences in Appearance

Sometimes children are left out because they don't look like the other children. Children of other races, children with physical disabilities, and children who are obese are sometimes treated cruelly. Children must learn to treat all other children with kindness and respect, but many of them still have a lot to learn. If your child's appearance sets him apart from his peer group, talk to your child's teacher and school counselor. They can often take a leadership role in helping the other children learn better social skills and behaviors.

Poor Sports

Children who are poor sports have trouble making friends. If your child cheats to win, if he won't play cooperatively, if he quits when he doesn't get his way or brags when he has success, you need to help him understand that his behaviors are getting in the way of his social relationships.

Examine your own competitiveness if your child is having trouble in this area. If you need to win at all costs or if your spouse feels compelled to win, your child has modeled his behavior directly.

You can help him understand the difference between boasting and expressions of joy over winning. Unfortunately, so many of today's sports heroes are poor models for this behavior. You may have to model the appropriate language, and you can help your child adjust his language by providing a suitable script.

Teach him to say, "That was a great game. I had a good time. Better luck next time."

Perhaps your child feels pressure to excel. Let him know you love him for who he is, not for how many points he can score. The strategies in chapter 8 designed to elevate self-esteem can help a child who is having trouble being a good sport.

Lying, cheating, and stealing are all behaviors that can have social causes and social consequences. Children who lie have trouble keeping friends. Friendship is based on trust, and children who lie can't be trusted. If you suspect your child is lying, look for the problems that are leading to the behavior. Is your child lying because he is afraid to tell the truth? This is more common in relationships with parents than with friends. It is more likely he is lying to boost his image with his peers. Children almost always get caught in their lies. This is so often an unsuccessful strategy that we might wonder why children try it. Children with low self-esteem sometimes need to lie about their achievements.

Sometimes children lie to protect their friends. Unfortunately, when they do they sometimes elevate their social position.

Children who steal also have social difficulties. Though older children might be involved in stealing as a social activity, younger children who steal are seldom admired by their peers. If your child is stealing, you need to have a discussion about personal property and the way someone feels when something is taken from him. Children who steal should be held accountable for their behavior. If your child steals, you should insist she return the stolen object.

If your child continues to lie or cheat or steal, seek professional help.

Negative Relationships

As we discussed in chapter 2, friendships can sometimes be negative. If you are unhappy with your child's choice of playmates, examine your concerns. Are you worried about them because of their clothes, or because of their activities? Are you troubled by their reputations? These issues can be a source of concern for parents of all children, but parents of adolescents have the most difficulty with this issue.

Watch what you say about your child's relationships. Sometimes our critical analysis of a child's peers creates even more interest in the forbidden fruit. Because your child has elected to be a part of a particular group, when you criticize your child's friends, you criticize him, too.

You can help your child find more positive role models by insisting he get involved in an activity that attracts children who are interested in more positive activities.

Remember, your child has a right to choose his own friends, but you have the obligation to intervene if your child puts himself in a dangerous situation.

If your child is having trouble making or keeping friends, it will affect his school life as well. Contact your child's teachers and school guidance counselors for support and advice. As we discussed in the previous chapter, school professionals can often structure social-skills groups where your child can learn how to behave in social situations.

CHAPTER 7

Getting Help

Mark's parents acknowledged the seriousness of his behavior when he set fire to a neighbor's house. Lexie's parents decided they needed help when she threatened to commit suicide. For Simone's parents, the process was more gradual. When she was little, they thought she was simply shy and fearful. She preferred to play alone and she did not like to be with strangers. She threw temper tantrums when she was left with a baby-sitter. Her parents thought she was going through a stage, but by the time she was thirteen, she refused to go to school. On the days her parents were able to get her there, she was in the nurse's office complaining of a stomachache within the first fifteen minutes. Her attendance record was so poor she was at risk of failing all of her subjects.

For most parents, the ordinary behavioral problems discussed in the early chapters of this book are the most serious they will ever have to face. For many other parents, however, serious emotional problems or behavioral disorders will disrupt their children's lives and, in the process, will turn their own lives upside down.

The disorders discussed in this section are serious and require the help of professionals; but despite the seriousness of the problems caused by emotional and behavioral disorders, most parents are uncomfortable making the decision to seek outside help. Often when counseling is suggested by schools, parents will say, "Oh, it's not *that* bad." The idea of therapy is often intimidating. Some parents are afraid a specialist will blame their child's behavior on them or else confirm their worst fears and recommend medication or hospitalization. Many parents feel they have somehow failed their child or are somehow to blame for their child's difficulties. Others worry their parenting skills will be judged as inadequate. In fact, the best parenting skills *are* inadequate in the face of many of these serious behavioral problems.

Handling a child's behavioral or emotional problem is one of the most difficult challenges parents will face. But when a child is in crisis, parents must get beyond these issues in order to help. If your child's behavior doesn't feel right, do something about it.

Look at your child's behavior as objectively as possible and consider whether it is age appropriate. While it is not unusual for a two-year-old to have a temper tantrum when he doesn't get his way, it is more unusual to have repeated tantrums from a five-year-old.

Consider the length of time your child's behavior has been a problem. All children go through normal developmental stages when behavior is less than desirable; but if your child is going though a prolonged period of inappropriate behavior and recommended modifications in your discipline strategy provide no relief, your child may have a more serious problem.

Indicators of a serious problem usually become obvious at home or at school. If your child's behavior is making your home life unbearable, or if you are receiving repeated reports from school about your child, chances are you and your child are going to need professional help.

Examine the severity of your child's behavior and mood. All children get into spats with friends and siblings. However, if your child is violent and overly aggressive or is withdrawn and has lost interest in his friends or favorite activities, he may need to see a mental health professional.

Sometimes changes in behavior come as a result of a situational crisis. A death or serious illness in the family, a divorce, frequent moves, or a change in schools can create stress in children that can be alleviated by short-term counseling. Often, however, these issues are not related to a specific situation and will require long-term treatment.

Usually parents have a sense that something is wrong, but they don't trust their own instincts. Husbands and wives might argue about whether counseling is in order. When one parent feels it is and the other disagrees, it is difficult to follow through on the conviction. If you need help convincing yourself or your spouse that your child and your family are in need of counseling, you might enlist the help of the many professionals who can help you sort it out.

However, some behaviors are so serious that parents should seek professional help immediately. Seek help now if your child:

- is self-abusive.
- talks or writes about hurting himself or someone else.
- puts himself in harmful situations (like deliberately running in front of a car).
- abuses animals.
- sets fires.
- becomes violent or uses weapons.
- is obsessed about weight and refuses to eat, or eats obsessively.
- is severely withdrawn or depressed.
- becomes destructive.
- engages in unsafe sexual activity.
- abuses drugs, including alcohol.

We have included in this chapter some of the most common disorders affecting child behavior. Though the problems are serious, the good news is that today these disorders are recognized earlier, and many respond to treatment.

Emotional and Behavioral Disorders

Listed below are the most common emotional and behavioral disorders that affect children. If your child is exhibiting these behaviors, see your doctor for a complete evaluation. For many of the disorders in this section, we have adapted the list of symptoms from the *Diagnostic and Statistical Manual for Mental Disorders*, fourth edition (DSM-IV). Explore this section if your child is exhibiting behaviors you suspect may be indicators of a serious problem.

Appendix C contains names and addresses of agencies offering guidance and support in your efforts to help your child, as well as recommended reading for additional information.

Alcohol and Drug Abuse

Alcohol and drug use and abuse are far too common behaviors in our children, and children are beginning to experiment with alcohol and drugs at younger and younger ages. Recent data released by the two groups who regularly monitor drug and alcohol use in the United States, the Substance Abuse and Mental Health Services Administration (SAMHSA) and the National Institute on Drug Abuse (NIDA), provide reasons for parents to be concerned. The surveys indicate that 40 percent of sixth graders have tried beer or wine. More alarming is the fact that 15 percent of eighth graders reported having five or more drinks in the two weeks before they were surveyed. Therefore, this alcohol use is not the "one beer in the parking lot" use most parents believe their children may be experiencing. Many adolescents and preadolescents are drinking regularly. This may lead to the alarming statistic that there are 4.4 million binge drinkers and 1.9 million heavy drinkers under the age of twenty-one.

Surveys also indicate that this generation of baby boomer parents often does not view the use of drugs and/or alcohol as a significant problem. For this reason, we are including in this section the reasons why parents should be concerned about the use of drugs and alcohol.

Why the Concern?

These substances place children at a high risk for injury and death and may affect cognitive and emotional development as well. Alcohol consumption plays a role in one-half of motor vehicle accidents and homicides among adolescents, and 30 percent of adolescent suicides involve the use of alcohol or other drugs. When adolescents drown, fall, or are injured in fires, alcohol is often a factor. Children who take the risk of using drugs and alcohol often enjoy the thrill of all sorts of risky behaviors.

Children who abuse alcohol and drugs have higher levels of truancy, fighting, and delinquency. They have shorter attention spans, are more easily distracted, show poor judgment, have impaired communication skills, are less mature, and are less effective in social situations.

Alcohol and drug use is often perceived as a normal part of growing up. But that very use is contributing to abuse and addiction in our children. A recent survey in middle America indicated that 11 percent of ninth grade students and 23 percent of twelfth grade students met formal diagnostic criteria for drug abuse or drug dependence disorder.

To complicate matters further, children are sometimes using alcohol or drugs or both to self-medicate. These children have other disorders in their lives that are actually driving them to search for a way to cope. Children with depression or with conduct disorders are looking for ways to help them feel better. Too often alcohol and drug use or abuse may be recognized, but the underlying disorder that led to the abuse is missed.

Children with learning disabilities or attention deficit disorders may use drugs to deal with the frustrations caused by their special challenges. Children with a family history of alcohol and drug abuse are at an increased risk for developing problems with both.

Many of the symptoms of alcohol and drug use overlap symptoms of other disorders in this section. If your child displays any of these signs, she may have a problem with drugs or alcohol.

- Problems at school, including poor attendance, falling grades
- Problems violating rules and regulations—school rules, household rules, laws
- Signs of depression: depressed mood, changes in weight, sleep problems, mood swings, suicidal thoughts
- Problems with concentration
- Hostility
- Changes in relationships with family members or friends
- Loss of interest in activities
- Red eyes; runny nose
- Stealing; household money is missing
- Physical evidence—pipes, papers, small medicine bottles, eye drops, etc

The abuse of alcohol and drugs can create major behavioral problems at home and at school and it places a high level of stress on families. If your child is exhibiting the above behaviors, they are probably having a major impact on you and your family. Because the use of alcohol and drugs so often muddles thinking, children and adolescents often do not recognize the seriousness of their behavior. Discuss the problem openly with your child when she is sober, and try to remain calm. Let her know that her safety and well-being are your primary concern and that you care. Hold firm to your house rules, and follow through with your discipline.

Try to be objective. Many parents find it very difficult to believe that their child has an alcohol or drug problem. Look at the evidence, and don't make excuses. If your child's behavior indicates she may have a problem, seek help.

Children who have substance abuse problems will need treatment. Remember, this is an illness. Find a counselor who is experienced in the treatment of alcohol and drug problems and who has experience with family therapies. There have been many changes in family therapy over the past decade, and many families can benefit from this multidimensional approach. Therapists are not out to place blame on parents but recognize that family is one of the most important influences on a child. Changes in family dynamics can play a part in the successful treatment of a child. This type of counseling can help open family communication and provide guidance and support for the family that is struggling to cope with this disease.

Sometimes parents will be involved in a less structured way. The child may receive individual or group therapy, and the family will occasionally meet with the therapist to receive information, learn strategies to help support the patient, and help them be more knowledgeable in the long-range treatment of the problem.

Occasionally, an older child's addictions can be treated with individual counseling, but most often the family will be involved. Seek recommendations from your pediatrician or a school counselor, or use the services of one of the agencies listed in appendix C to help you find the right person to help your child and your family.

Children with addictions may be treated in outpatient programs, with medication, and/or in residential programs.

The use of medications in the treatment of drug and alcohol dependency and abuse is complicated by the fact that so many who need treatment have other disorders as well. The treatment of the underlying disorder often produces beneficial results in treating the abuse of alcohol or drugs. As we mentioned earlier, children and adolescents may be using illegal drugs or alcohol in an effort to treat themselves. Many of the drugs used to treat depression, anxiety, and conduct disorders are helpful when treating addictions that have underlying disorders. Stimulants, antidepressants, lithium, and valproic acid are among the drugs sometimes used in the treatment of adolescents. (See the "Pharmacology" section of this chapter for more information about specific drugs). Because there can be serious drug interactions between prescribed medications and illegal drugs such as marijuana, careful medical supervision is essential when treating alcohol and drug problems.

You will find a list of resources providing additional information on alcohol and drug abuse and dependence in appendix C.

Anxiety Disorders

Most children experience anxious moments while growing up. Young children are often anxious when their parents leave. Many adolescents are nervous when they have to speak in front of the class. Children with anxiety disorders, however, are overwhelmed by their feelings. Their responses are excessive and illogical. Some children also manifest physical symptoms related to their level of anxiety. What differentiates anxiety disorders from common nervous feelings is the degree of anxiety. Children with anxiety disorders are often burdened with a sense of overwhelming fear or a sense of impending doom. Anxiety disorders can be incapacitating and can prevent children from performing everyday activities and from developing and maintaining relationships with other children and adults. Obviously these types of fears have a profound impact on a child's behavior. Depending on the specific disorder, children may avoid new situations, refuse to go to school, refuse to speak, or refuse to see their friends. They may have disrupted sleep and nightmares, or they may be unable to concentrate. They may be obsessed with endless washing or counting.

There are several types of anxiety disorders, and many children with one of these disorders have others as well—a condition professionals refer to as comorbidity. Many children with anxiety disorders also suffer from depression (see "Depression" in this chapter). What follows is a brief explanation of these disorders and the types of treatment that might be recommended for them. Remember these are serious issues, and though they require the cooperation of parents during treatment, children with these disorders must be assessed and treated by a professional.

Generalized Anxiety Disorder (GAD)

According to the National Institute of Mental Health (NIMH), GAD is chronic and exaggerated worry and tension, even though nothing seems to provoke it. There is no one specific trigger for this type of anxiety. Children with GAD are worriers, and they worry excessively about things other children would never consider as troublesome. They worry about things they have done in the past, and they often worry even more about what might happen in the future. Frequently, they are self-conscious and in need of constant reassurance. Children with GAD find it extremely difficult to relax, thus giving rise to physical symptoms such as irritability, twitching, muscle tension, headaches, stomachaches, nausea, trouble sleeping, and others. These symptoms continue for long periods of time and may be diagnosed when they last for more than six months. Many children with GAD also have ADHD, separation anxiety disorder, phobias, and/or depression.

Treatment for this condition may include cognitive-behavioral therapy; relaxation techniques, including breathing exercises; and biofeedback to control muscle tension. Children may be encouraged to imagine safe and comfortable situations and to practice recalling the feeling they have there when faced with feelings of anxiety. GAD may also be treated with a medication called buspirone.

Separation Anxiety Disorder (SAD)

Separation anxiety is probably the most easily recognized by parents. As we mentioned earlier, it isn't unusual for young children to worry about being separated from their parents. When this behavior extends beyond the normal developmental age (beyond the beginning of kindergarten), however, a serious disorder may be present. When a child's normal activities and family life are impaired by her anxiety over separation, and when the anxiety has continued for more than a month, an evaluation is in order. Children suffering from SAD exhibit several of the following symptoms for more than a month:

- Excessive and unrealistic fear of being separated from their parents (particularly mothers) or primary caregivers, or from their homes
- Unrealistic fear that they or their parents will become ill or be harmed or injured in some way if they are separated
- Refusal to go to school

- Refusal to sleep alone or away from home, or has nightmares about separation
- Avoidance of being alone
- Fear of getting lost
- Physical symptoms of anxiety when they anticipate leaving home or separating from their parents: stomachaches, headaches, vomiting.

Children with separation anxiety may respond to psychotherapy including play therapy and behavior therapy (desensitization or exposure); moreover, some medications can significantly reduce anxiety enough for children to leave home.

Specific Phobia

Specific phobia, sometimes referred to as simply phobia, is an unrealistic and debilitating fear of specific objects or situations that lasts for more than six months. When confronted with this feared object or situation, the child experiences extreme distress and, as a result, avoids the object or situation. This avoidance behavior interferes with a child's normal ability to function.

Specific phobia can include a fear of specific creatures (dogs, cats, insects, etc.), a particular environment (heights, escalators, water, etc.), or a particular situation (such as being excessively fearful of blood or injections). What makes this disorder particularly difficult is that children rarely recognize just how irrational their fears are. Children who suffer from specific phobia express their fears by crying, throwing tantrums, freezing, or clinging.

Most children outgrow their unrealistic fears, but if the phobia continues for more than six months, a treatment program may be helpful. Behavior therapy (including desensitization or exposure), group therapy, play therapy, and certain medications can help with the anxiety associated with specific phobia.

Panic Disorders/Agoraphobia

Young people with panic disorders experience panic attacks that terrorize them. These attacks often come unexpectedly and provoke both physical and psychological symptoms. According to the NIMH, physical symptoms may include:

- pounding heart, chest pains, lightheadedness or dizziness, nausea or stomach problems, flushes or chills, shortness of breath or a feeling of smothering or choking, tingling or numbness, shaking or trembling, sweating
- feelings of unreality or terror
- feelings of being out of control or going crazy
- fear of dying

While panic disorders have been diagnosed in children as young as eight, adolescence is the most common time for the diagnosis of panic disorders.

Those with panic disorders often become afraid to go places where they might have a panic attack, fearing they might not be able to escape. They are afraid they might be embarrassed or that treatment might not be available to them. As a result, they avoid places where they do not feel safe. This avoidance behavior so restricts those with panic disorders that they cannot live normal lives. Once the disorder has escalated to this level, it is called agoraphobia.

Cognitive/behavior therapy, medication, or a combination of the two may be used to treat agoraphobia. In cognitive/behavior therapy, children may learn to use breathing exercises to help them relax, or they may learn skills that help them refocus their attention in order to help alleviate the feelings of anxiety. Medications including antidepressants may help.

Social Phobia

Children suffering with social phobia worry excessively about social situations or about having to perform in public. They are fearful of public scrutiny and the possibility of embarrassment or humiliation. Most often this disorder is diagnosed during early adolescence, but it can be a problem for younger children as well. For example, children with this disorder might avoid eating in the cafeteria, or they may become extremely anxious when an oral report is assigned. This anxiety is not caused by shyness. Shy people may be uneasy around others, but they do not experience the symptoms of serious anxiety when they are with other people, and they may not alter their lives in response to their fears.

This phobia, like the other disorders in this section, can interfere with a child's life. She may avoid school in order to avoid giving that oral report. He might go to the nurse's office at lunchtime so he doesn't have to eat in public.

Often children have no control over the social situations in which they are placed and may cry, throw tantrums, cling to their parents, or refuse to participate in group play. As they grow older, they may refuse to go to school or participate in age-appropriate activities, like school trips or dances.

Sometimes social phobias have specific triggers. A child may be embarrassed after vomiting in class or tripping while entering a classroom. The embarrassment is so extreme that the child can no longer put himself at risk of another embarrassing moment.

Those who were excessively afraid of new situations or were extremely shy when they were younger are more likely to develop social phobia, and those children whose parents had social anxieties are also more likely to have social phobia. Children with social phobia may also suffer from depression.

Children may find relief from their symptoms when treated with cognitive/behavior therapy and/or medications. In treating a child with social phobia, the therapist might use a form of exposure therapy. The child might be exposed to an anxiety-provoking situation by imagining it and gradually allowing the anxiety level to decrease. She can visit this imagined place and have the safety of leaving it and returning to the therapist's office, which gives the child a great deal of control—something she often feels is lacking in her confrontations with her fears. The child is systematically desensitized to the anxiety-provoking situations until she is able to tackle the actual situation. Drug therapies are sometimes used in conjunction with cognitive/behavior therapy.

Selective Mutism

Selective mutism is a specific type of social phobia and affects a very small number of children (fewer than 1 percent). Children with this disorder refuse to speak in specific social situations but will speak in other settings. A child with selective mutism, for example, may refuse to talk at school but will speak to family and close friends at home. The child might also speak in an altered voice or in a whisper in some situations. Children with this disorder usually have normal communication and social skills in comfortable environments, and observers would not suspect that this same child could possibly be silent in another setting.

Children with this disorder have a history of shyness around strangers, and when looking back on the child's behavior, parents often acknowledge that the child may not have actually spoken to anyone outside the family for a long period of time. Because young children may spend much of their day in a "closed" environment (with family and friends), the symptoms present no major problem until the child enters school.

It is important to note that this disorder does not stem from disobedience or from willful conduct on the child's part.

A child with selective mutism doesn't speak because she is extremely anxious and fearful of speaking. Some children with this disorder manage to communicate with gestures (nodding, pointing), in facial expressions, in writing, or with grunts. Some remain expressionless until others guess what they are trying to communicate.

Assuming the child speaks the prevalent language or is not hiding a communication disorder such as stuttering, the criteria for selective mutism include:

- failure to speak in specific school situations, despite speaking in other situations
- developmental delay in school achievement or social communication
- mutism lasting for at least one month (other than the first month of school)
- symptoms not caused by psychotic disorder

The cause of selective mutism has not been established, but children with this specific form of social phobia often have parents who suffer similar anxiety disorders—extreme shyness, social phobia, or other anxiety disorders.

Children with this disorder may need professional help and often benefit from behavioral and/or play therapy that includes a transition from nonverbal play to play that includes speaking. Some therapy includes a strategy called stimulus fading, in which the child and his parent speak together. The teacher joins the two and gradually enters into the conversation. If the child is engaged in the conversation, the parent gradually stops talking. Once communication with a person outside the family is established, another person may be introduced, a classmate, for example.

Strategies for the treatment of this disorder are as individual as each child and may involve the help of therapists, counselors, language specialists, teachers, and even medical personnel. (Medications used most often to reduce anxiety are phenelzine and fluoxetine.)

Because most children with selective mutism do not speak in school settings, parents must work closely with teachers, school pscyhologists, and occupational therapists to develop a treatment plan.

Think of this disorder as your child's silent scream for help. Find as much information as you can on the subject and share it with all those who work with your child. The diagnosis of selective mutism is sometimes delayed, and a child may be ridiculed, punished, or reprimanded for not speaking. This only increases her level of anxiety and makes the situation worse.

Parents can encourage the child to widen her speaking environment to include less familiar relatives. They can help foster the development of friendships among a small group of friends who attend the child's school. Sometimes children can make the transition between talking to those close friends at home and at school. This provides opportunity for the child to interact in normal situations within the school setting. Praise any small accomplishments in the child's efforts to speak. In particular, reward charts can help reinforce positive gains as the child begins to speak outside the home. Because this disorder can have a major impact on a child's social and educational progress at school, seek help if your child displays the symptoms of this disorder for more than a month.

Obsessive Compulsive Disorder (OCD)

Children with OCD have recurrent and persistent ideas or thoughts that get in the way of their day-to-day activities and/or they perform rituals or repetitive activities that also interfere with normal activities. The most common of these compulsions stem from a fear of germs or contamination. The idea or thought of being contaminated (the obsession) is so powerful it leads to a ritual or compulsion, usually involving washing and cleaning. Also high on the list of rituals or compulsions are checking or counting. A child may come to believe the old rhyme, *step on a crack; you break your mother's back*. Once again, the thought or idea provokes the ritual. A child may count all the cracks in the sidewalk between home and school to consistently avoid them. If anything interrupts the count, he must return home and start again. In fact, the fear of harming themselves or someone they love is one of the most common obsessions in children with this disorder.

The rituals involved in OCD can be so time-consuming that they take up a significant amount of a child's time. The rituals can interfere in school when what would be a normal activity for a typical child, such as turning off the lights, turns out to be a ritual for the child. He may not be able to just turn the light off. He may fear that someone will come to harm if he just turns it off once. He is compelled to turn it off twenty times. It is very unusual for a child to have an obsession without a ritual to address it, and many children with this disorder perform multiple rituals.

Adults with OCD usually recognize that the rituals and obsessions are senseless, but they still have difficulty controlling them. Children, however, often do not recognize the senselessness of their fears. Children as young as nine have been reported with symptoms of this disorder, and in children, it is most often diagnosed in the preteen to early teenage years.

Current evidence suggests this disorder may run in families. Brain imaging studies of OCD show abnormal neurochemical activity levels in regions of the brain known to play a role in certain neurological disorders. OCD is often accompanied by other anxiety disorders, and sometimes young people with OCD also have eating disorders.

Cognitive/behavior psychotherapy may be helpful with OCD. This therapy exposes the child to objects that create anxiety until the anxiety passes and helps them learn to refrain from rituals. This type of therapy also helps those with OCD clarify and modify the thoughts that lead to the obsessions and rituals.

Medications may be recommended in serious cases of OCD, especially if cognitive/behavior therapy alone is unsuccessful. Medications that affect serotonin levels, such as clomipramine and fluvoxamine, have been approved by the FDA for use in children and may be helpful in the treatment of OCD.

There are several strategies to try at home to help you and your child cope with this disorder. Because rituals and obsessions can dominate your child's life, it is likely that it will cause some disruptions in your family. Family therapy can often help children, their siblings, and their parents cope.

It is impossible to ignore your child's behaviors, so acknowledge them. Instead of saying, "Stop doing that," you might say, "I see you are feeling anxious and need to touch the doorknob." This gives your child an opening to talk about her ritual in a supportive environment. When your child tries and succeeds at resisting a compulsion, be sure to notice and to praise her for her efforts.

Try to remain calm and kind in the face of this disorder. Your child finds it impossible to control her behavior and needs your support; and while you might find her behaviors very upsetting, remember, your child is much more upset by her behavior than you are.

Be sure to work with the professionals at your child's school. An informed teacher and counselor can help your child during the time she is away from you.

Post-Traumatic Stress Disorder (PTSD)

Unlike other anxiety disorders, PTSD has a specific, often identifiable cause. Children with PTSD are reacting to a terrifying event and believe they and/or others are in jeopardy.

This disorder occurs in response to seeing or experiencing physical abuse, sexual abuse, violence in the community or in the family, severe accidents or disasters, life-threatening illnesses, and war.

Children with PTSD reexperience the triggering event, often through sleep disorders and nightmares. In very young children, the nightmares may change from specific dreams about the event to more generalized dreams of monsters or other frightening creatures. During the day, disturbing memories or flashbacks of the event can be stressful to older children. Young children may reenact the event with their dolls or toys during play. Older children will try to avoid anything that reminds them of the event. In all cases, PTSD hinders the child's ability to concentrate.

One of the most disturbing symptoms of PTSD is that children don't believe they will live into adulthood. As a result, children with PTSD may become disinterested in things that once gave them pleasure. They may be irritable, aggressive, and sometimes violent. It is important to note that not all children who experience traumatic events have PTSD, and diagnosis is usually made if symptoms last for more than a month.

At home, parents should let children know that it is okay to talk about the traumatic event and encourage them to talk. If symptoms of PTSD develop and continue, seek the help of a professional.

Treatment of PTSD may include cognitive/behavior or family therapy, and in cases of serious anxiety, medication. Specialists in the field of PTSD may help your child remember the events in a safe environment, help her with relationships with family and friends, and help her deal with the anger, depression, and anxiety that is associated with this disorder.

Parents dealing with the anxiety disorders in this chapter need support systems to help them help their children. Find a support group, either at your child's school, through your community mental health center, or online. Resources can be found in appendix C.

Disruptive Behavior Disorders

Attention Deficit Hyerpactivity Disorder (ADHD)

ADHD is one of the most common behavior disorders among children and one of the problems that often leads to difficulty in school. ADHD affects 3 to 5 percent of all children, and many of them have other disorders or learning disabilities in combination with ADHD.

In recent years, there has been much discussion in schools and in the media regarding the misdiagnosis, overdiagnosis, and overtreatment of children with this disorder. However, a recent report in the *Journal of the American Medical Association* takes issue with those anecdotal reports. After reviewing and analyzing twenty-two years of studies about children with ADHD and the use of stimulants to treat the disorder, Larry S. Goldman, M.D., and other researchers from the Council on Scientific Affairs of the American Medical Association found little evidence of widespread overdiagnosis or misdiagnosis or overtreatment with stimulant medication.

The symptoms of ADHD fall into two broad categories: ADHD with inattention and ADHD with a display of hyperactivity and impulsivity. Though more boys than girls are diagnosed with ADHD, some researchers feel more girls may have ADHD with inattention characteristics and go unidentified because they do not cause a disruption in the classroom. A child with ADHD and inattention:

- fails to give attention to details; makes careless mistakes;
- has difficulty sustaining attention in school or recreational activities;
- has poor listening skills; doesn't seem to be listening;

- fails to follow directions or to complete tasks;
- has poor organizational skills;
- avoids tasks that require mental effort (schoolwork, homework);
- misplaces items needed for school or for play;
- is easily distracted; and
- is forgetful.

Children with these qualities obviously have difficulty in school. Often their problems are viewed as laziness or intentional inattention, and it may take longer for parents and teachers to recognize these children as needing an evaluation for this disorder.

Children with the hyperactivity/impulsivity criteria are difficult to miss, as suggested by the following:

Hyperactivity
- Fidgets and wiggles and squirms
- Has trouble staying seated
- Runs about or climb inappropriately
- Has difficulty doing quiet activities
- Is "on the go"
- Talks excessively

Impulsivity
- Blurts out answers
- Has trouble taking turns and waiting for turns
- Interrupts others

Children diagnosed with ADHD display six or more of these symptoms. They also show the following signs:

- Inattentive, hyperactive, or impulsive behaviors before the age of seven
- Impaired achievement at home, in work situations, or in social situations

- Behavior display in more than one setting, and continuing for at least six months

As a result of their behaviors, children with ADHD often experience peer rejection, have difficulty with academic performance, and get into trouble at school and in the community. As we mentioned earlier, children with ADHD often have other disabling problems including depression, conduct disorder, and a susceptibility to drug and alcohol addiction and abuse. If your child is experiencing difficulty in school or at home and displays more that six of these symptoms, consult a professional to determine if your child may have ADHD.

No one knows what causes ADHD, but current evidence suggests it may involve abnormalities in activity levels in the areas of the brain that control attention and inhibit impulses. The disorder seems to be hereditary. Children with ADHD usually have at least one close relative with the disorder, and at least one-third of the fathers who had ADHD as children have children who also have ADHD. A majority of identical twins share the disorder.

Unlike other conduct disorders, there is no evidence of a relationship between the home environment and the development of ADHD. Children from stable homes and children from unstable homes can develop the disorder.

Treatment has become a hot button in many settings. Whether or not to medicate, whether the drugs can be abused, whether they should be prescribed as long as the child has symptoms, or whether they should be discontinued as a child ages are all topics of conversation among parents and educators. Theories for alternative treatments range from special diets to special glasses.

Cheryl and I do not make medical recommendations. Those decisions should be made with a medical professional or specialist in the treatment of ADHD. We can, however, provide some information to help you in your discussions with professionals.

Medical experts in the field acknowledge they still do not know enough about the disorder and that there have been few long-term clinical studies of the effect of drugs in treating ADHD. However, short-term clinical trials of stimulant medications (methylphenidate, dextroamphetamine, pemoline) provide evidence that medications are more effective than behavioral therapies in reducing some of the symptoms of ADHD, as long as the medication is taken. Nine out of ten children show improvement on one of the stimulant drugs when it is properly administered and supervised. (Though the NIMH considers these medications quite safe, they have side effects.) Antidepressants and other medications may be used to help control accompanying depression or anxiety and drugs used to treat hypertension may be beneficial for children who have both ADHD and Tourette syndrome.

Though drugs can dramatically reduce hyperactivity symptoms, improve attention, and may help control impulsivity, they are not a cure. Treatment with drugs alone does not address the issues of low self-esteem so often experienced by children with ADHD, nor do they address the emotional needs of the children or the adults who live and work with them. Moreover, behavior therapies and parent training help provide a more productive school environment and a less stressful home environment. Both are essential in dealing with this disorder.

Though there have been many anecdotal reports of improvements with alternative therapies including dietary plans, vitamin supplements, motion sickness medication, treatment of candida yeast, biofeedback, chiropractic treatment, and vision training, no clinical studies of alternative therapies have been conducted, and there is no medical evidence that these are beneficial in treating ADHD.

If your child has symptoms of ADHD and is having trouble at home, at school, or in social situations, seek the help of a professional who has experience in treating children with this disorder. Many pediatricians today are experienced in the treatment of ADHD and there are mental health professionals who focus their practices on the treatment of children with this disorder. Let them help you make decisions about medications and therapies.

If your child has already been diagnosed with ADHD, you probably already know about the stress that is involved in raising a child with this diagnosis. Raising a child is difficult under any circumstances, but raising a child with ADHD puts additional stress on the family. Loud voices, short tempers, and lots of guilt are common in homes of children with ADHD.

Parenting and discipline strategies can help make life at home less stressful. For most children, and especially for children with ADHD, structure and consistency are the keys. As much as possible, keep a predictable schedule—a time for meals, a time for homework, a time for bed. Though it is difficult to provide this kind of structure in today's hectic homes, it is worth the effort.

Children with ADHD need to know what you expect of them (your expectations must be realistic) and they need to know the consequences of both inappropriate behaviors and appropriate behaviors. Set your rules, post them as a reminder, and follow through with consequences.

Don't get into protracted arguments. Children with ADHD can be very skilled at arguing, and you will only end the argument more frustrated than when you began. You are in charge. Take control. Provide an uncluttered, quiet place for work, and have your child do his homework there.

Make time for your child. All children benefit from time with loving parents, but children with ADHD especially need your time. Set aside a period of time each day, at least twenty minutes, to spend some time with your child. Go for a walk together, share a snack, and take time to talk. During this special time, be sure to focus on the positive things that have happened during the day. You can even direct the conversation. Ask, "What was the best thing that happened today?" Use this as an opportunity for praise. There are enough difficult times during the day for a child with ADHD.

Use an "early warning" system. Children with ADHD have major difficulties during times of transition. Let them know well in advance when it is getting close to bedtime or time for dinner. Give them a time frame. For example, "We will be having dinner in fifteen minutes, so you should begin cleaning up your toys."

Keep your eyes on your child. Not necessarily to observe them for transgressions, but to let them you know you care about them. Eye contact can bring a child back from a daydream with less stress than a shout or a poke and your glance gives him a quiet message that you are there and care about him.

Lists are also very helpful. Assignment notebooks help children remember homework tasks, and posting schedules of all kinds help them remember what they are supposed to be doing and when.

All children benefit from regular exercise, and children with ADHD need it more than most. Aerobic exercise, in particular, can get rid of pent-up energy and relieve stress. Many children with ADHD find team sports difficult, but individual performance sports like running, bicycling, skating, etc., can provide emotional and physical benefits.

Though it is hard to relax in a home with a child with ADHD, try to enjoy the qualities of your child that make him so special. Children with ADHD can be very difficult, but they can also be very creative. Many children with ADHD love music and musical messages. Sing your requests to your child, deliver your message in rhyme, or add some humor by asking for cooperation in a silly voice. If you can make your child laugh and you can laugh with him, you not only alleviate the anxiety of the moment but you provide loving memories for the future.

Avoid overstimulating activities. Wild television programs, loud music, simultaneous noise and activities, and too many playmates can provoke hyperactive and impulsive symptoms in children with ADHD. Provide entertaining environments, but don't go too far.

Break it up; the work, that is. Large tasks and long-term assignments are often overwhelming. Help your child divide tasks into manageable chunks and praise him as he completes each step of the task. As he completes each part, he will begin to see that even major assignments can be handled one step at a time.

Repeat yourself. Yes, in this case it can be a positive thing. Children with ADHD often have difficulty remembering instructions. Complicated instructions are even more difficult. In school we say, "tell them what you are going to teach, teach it, and tell them what you have taught." The same strategy works at home.

Watch for complications. Children with ADHD often have more than one disorder. If your child begins to exhibit signs of depression, oppositional disorder, or Tourette syndrome, consult your doctor.

Nurture, nurture, nurture. Children with ADHD experience failure in school and social situations more often than any of us like to acknowledge. Make your home a place to celebrate accomplishments, to encourage further achievements, and to nurture your child with praise and affection.

One of the most important things you can do for a child with ADHD is to take care of yourself. Children with ADHD can cause extreme levels of stress that can lead to marital distress, alcohol and drug abuse, and unfortunately child abuse. Though there is no evidence that stressful home situations cause ADHD, they can contribute to other emotional disorders such as depression and conduct disorder. It is in your child's best interest for you to be in a strong emotional state in order to help him. Research shows that parents who had ADHD as a child or who have attention problems as adults often have the most difficulty helping children with the disorder. If you feel overwhelmed, don't hesitate to ask for help.

Both individual and family counseling can be helpful when raising a child with ADHD, and talking with others who are also raising children with the disorder can help relieve parent anxiety and can often provide tips to help you in your relationship with your child. Most schools have support groups for parents and Web sites are now available for parents to chat with anonymity. We have listed several resources in appendix C.

Oppositional Defiant Disorder and Conduct Disorder

Two of the most troubling disorders in young children and adolescents are oppositional defiant disorder (ODD) and conduct disorder (CD). These two disorders seem to create more stress in families than any other behavioral problem. When children with these disorders also have attention deficit disorders or depression, the level of stress skyrockets.

The diagnosis of these disorders is often complicated by the very symptoms of the disorders themselves. Children with ODD and CD can be extremely uncooperative.

Children with ODD are extremely difficult to get along with and to like. They are unusually argumentative and irritable, have short tempers, and frequently get into arguments with authority figures. They often blame others for their own mistakes. They frequently use obscene language and can be angry, resentful, spiteful, and vindictive. To make matters worse, they seem to behave this way on purpose. All children occasionally exhibit one of these behaviors, but when more than a few of these behaviors occur for more than six months, a child may have ODD. Unlike children with ADHD, children with ODD are not impulsive. Their behavior is intentional and often aggressive. Arguments are frequent in homes of children with ODD.

Unfortunately, ODD may affect as many as 5 percent of children. And to make matters worse, it is unusual to have only ODD. Many children with ODD often have attention deficit disorder, depression, or anxiety disorders. Those with ADHD and ODD can be particularly difficult and aggressive.

Because children with ODD seem to enjoy seeing parents and authority figures get upset, it is important to stay calm. Children with this disorder benefit from clear rules and consequences and from consistency.

Choose your battles. When noncompliance is a part of a child's personality, you can't give equal importance to a variety of infractions. Rules should be very specific and direct—no fighting, no swearing, and both negative and positive consequences should be part of the discipline plan. Reward good behaviors and discipline undesired behavior.

As with ADHD, reminders and early warnings help children with ODD transition from one activity to another.

Try to avoid power struggles. Children with ODD resent demands and may respond more favorably when given the power to make some decisions themselves. In that case, give them a choice. For example, ask, "Would you like to do your homework now, or would you rather wait until after dinner."

As we mentioned earlier in the ADHD section, parenting children with behavioral disorders can be extremely challenging and stressful. Take care of yourself. Build some exercise into your day and try to find time to talk to friends. Sometimes a sympathetic ear can make a difficult day more tolerable. Enlist the support of your spouse, and work together to help your child. Get lots of sleep. Many parents of oppositionally defiant children need professional assistance. Don't be embarrassed to admit it. Seek help.

Children with ODD and their families may benefit from therapy. Most often parents need assistance in learning new strategies for working with children with this disorder, and children need help dealing with their anger. Untreated, ODD can progress into the more serious behavior disorder, CD, discussed below. Family therapy, behavioral therapy, and psychotherapy may be useful in the treatment of this disorder, but parent training provides the adults with specific behavioral techniques to help maintain control in the relationship with the child. Drug treatment may be recommended for serious oppositional defiant disorders and may be used to treat other disorders including depression, ADHD, and anxiety. Clonidine is sometimes prescribed in the treatment of ODD.

Children with CD display even more disturbing behaviors than those with ODD. Often they are aggressive, physically dangerous, and destructive, displaying a level of cruelty not present in children with ODD. Symptoms include a repetitive and persistent pattern of behavior including the following:

- Serious aggression
    threatens or causes physical harm to people or animals
    initiates physical fights; may use weapons
    forces someone into sexual activity

- Destruction of Property
    firesetting
    vandalism
    breaking and entering into homes, cars, buildings

- Serious violation of rules
    lying
    stealing, including shoplifting
    running away from home
    truancy
    repeated curfew violations

Children with this disorder are often skillful liars who misrepresent the cause of their behavior, thus averting diagnosis. Their behavior is often so upsetting that it sparks anger and frustration in those very people working to help. Like other disruptive behavior disorders, children with CD often have multiple disorders (most often ADHD), and many have substance abuse problems.

Alarming statistics suggest this is a prevalent disorder in young people—from 6 to 16 percent of boys, and from 2 to 9 percent of girls. Children with CD often come from troubled homes, and unfortunately, violence may be a way of life for some of them. Most have experienced school failure, abusive family relationships, neglect, or brain damage; and they may have mental and emotional developmental problems as well. Not all come from abusive homes, however, and sometimes peer relationships are powerful enough to influence this behavior.

Behavioral therapy and individual psychotherapy may help a child learn to control his anger. In any case, children with this disorder and their families need long-term, comprehensive therapy. Parents, in particular, need to be directly involved in therapy as well and may benefit from management techniques to help them help their child. Professionals working with the child will need to get information from many of the adults involved in the child's life—parents, teachers, physicians, social service workers, and law enforcement personnel. As a last resort, children with CD sometimes need to be hospitalized or treated in institutional settings.

Prescription medicines may be used to control comorbid disorders. Stimulants, antidepressants, lithium carbonate, or carbamazipine may be used to treat associated ADHD, depression, or anxiety disorders. Resources may be found in appendix C.

Depression

Looking back on our lives as children, we often selectively remember the happy times—playing with friends, going on family trips, holiday celebrations, and so on. But if we take a minute to really think, most of us can remember hurtful and upsetting times as well—that time we weren't invited to a birthday party, when classmates made fun of us, when we failed to make an athletic team, or our hearts were broken by a boyfriend or girlfriend. While some adults dwell on such events and the long-term depression they precipitated, most of us got over that sadness and moved on.

Childhood, and especially adolescence, can be a very difficult time. So difficult, in fact, that according to the NIMH, 2.5 percent of children and 8.5 percent of adolescents in the United States suffer from depression. Depression can be a serious mental illness, and yet it is often missed entirely or misdiagnosed. The symptoms of depression can sometimes be misidentified as normal adolescent mood swings, and in some forms may be misdiagnosed in children as ADHD or ODD or CD.

To complicate matters, children suffering from many of the disorders we have discussed here may have a depressive illness as well. It is important to seek help if you suspect your child may be depressed because this illness can lead to more serious disorders as children and adolescents grow older; it often leads to difficulties at home and in school; and, most of all, at its most severe stages it may result in suicide attempts.

There are several types of depressive illnesses that may affect children, and while it is beyond the scope of this book to detail all of them, we have listed here the most common forms with brief explanations. Children who are depressed and/or who have the related illness, mania, display symptoms that affect the way they think, the way they behave and the way they feel, both physically and emotionally. These symptoms are not short-lived, and though they may go away for short periods of time, they come back again to interfere with a child's normal development and activities. Remember, the diagnosis of a mental illness must be made by a professional, and our goal here is to help you identify symptoms that may need further evaluation.

Major Depressive Disorder
Symptoms of major depressive disorder can include:

- profound sadness most of the time
- tearful most of the time or having a sad expression
- irritability
- excessive restlessness or excessive lethargy
- apathy
- problems with sleeping, including either difficulty sleeping or excessive sleeping
- problems with eating, including either loss of appetite or overeating
- feelings of hopelessness and despair
- feelings of low self-esteem; worthlessness
- feelings of shame
- inability to think clearly or to concentrate
- significant weight loss or weight gain
- loss of energy, chronic fatigue
- social withdrawal
- no longer enjoys or seeks out activities that once brought pleasure

- excessive guilt
- acting out
- suicidal or self-injurious thoughts or recurrent thoughts of death

Though it is not part of the specific criteria for diagnosing depression, depressed children often report physical complaints including headaches, stomachaches, dizziness, and others, as well. If your child experiences more than a few of the systems on the list above, and they continue for more than a couple of weeks, your child is probably having serious problems getting along at home and at school and should be evaluated by a professional. A child who has more than five of these symptoms at the same time may be suffering from major depressive disorder.

Dysthymic Disorder

Sometimes children appear to be depressed and display only two of these symptoms, but they continue for longer periods of time. If your child appears to be depressed and has more than two of these symptoms for more than a year, he may have a form of depression called dysthymic disorder and should be evaluated by a professional.

Double Depression

Children diagnosed with a dysthymic disorder may go on to develop a major depressive episode. When this happens, the illness is called double depression. When the major depressive episode abates, the child returns to the dysthymic state. This combination of depressive disorders can be very serious. Some children with dysthymia may also develop bipolar disorder.

Bipolar Disorder

Sometimes children with depression also have manic phases that alternate with periods of depression and periods of normal mood. Children with this illness go through marked mood swings from the extreme lows caused by depression to the extreme highs of manic phases. This disorder was once called manic-depressive disorder, but now is more often termed bipolar disorder. Children with this disorder may display several of the following symptoms between periods of depression:

- fast speech
- racing thoughts
- an unrealistic sense of well-being and feelings of superiority or invincibility
- elation, sometimes mixed with irritability
- impatience with those who do not think as quickly
- requiring little sleep
- impulsivity and/or poor judgment
- excessive involvement in pleasurable activities

Symptoms of this disorder may appear as young as the early teenage years, and because children often display the dangerous mix of feeling invincible and making poor decisions, young people with this illness often find themselves in trouble.

Cyclothymia

Children with cyclothymia exhibit fewer of the manic symptoms described above, but as in the dysthymic disorder, the symptoms last for longer periods of time. With this disorder, children experience "cycles" of elevated mood and periods of depressed mood. This pattern of mood swings must continue for at least one year in order for a diagnosis of cyclothymia to be made.

Research continues into the causes of depressive illnesses in children, but most today believe the illness results from a combination of factors including genetic, biochemical, and environmental factors. Children with a family history of depressive illness are more likely to suffer the symptoms of this disease. Researchers believe some children may have problems with the chemicals responsible for signaling from one nerve cell to another (neurotransmitters). Imbalances in these neurotransmitters can create mood disorders. Children who are exposed to ongoing stresses in their environment or who have suffered profound losses in their lives (either physical or emotional) are also at risk for this type of mental illness.

Any child who displays any of the symptoms that are life-threatening or who discusses taking her own life needs immediate medical attention. Depression can be an extremely serious illness, and any threat of suicide should be taken seriously.

Children who have experienced long or recurring symptoms of depression are more likely to experience severe or chronic depression, and the longer children suffer from depression, the more difficult it is to treat. For those reasons, parents should seek help for their children sooner rather than later.

Most children over the age of eight are treated in conjunction with their families in some form of family therapy. One such approach is cognitive/behavior therapy, which strives to make changes in the way the child thinks and feels. Since faulty thinking is often a problem for those who are depressed, the goal of therapy is to help correct or change the repetitive negative thoughts that can overwhelm. The therapist helps the child change the negative messages that go on inside his head into positive affirmations that help improve mood and self-esteem. Therapy might also address the child's social relationships through the development of appropriate social and communication skills.

Professionals in the field of mental health are also prepared to support and guide the entire family during the treatment of this difficult illness.

Antidepressant medications or lithium may be prescribed in the treatment of children with serious forms of depression.

A recent NIMH study supported fluoxetine, a selective serotonin reuptake inhibitor (SSRI), as safe and effective for children and adolescents with this condition. Studies are currently under way to study psychotropic medications in children and adolescents. An NIMH-funded study is also under way to investigate both medication and psychotherapeutic treatments for adolescent depression, so more information on this illness will be available in the near future.

At home, parents can try strategies designed to help children cope with their depression. Be a behavioral role model. Look for good things in your life, and talk about them each day. Some adults keep journals reflecting on the best things that happened each day. Encourage your child to do the same. Sometimes the negative factors in lives have a way of casting a shadow over everything—including the good things. Like the old song says, try to "look for the silver lining."

When those negative thoughts keep coming back, try to help your child think in a more rational way. Helping children overcome negative self-evaluations helps them help themselves overcome the thinking that contributes to low self-esteem. Recognize that your child has difficulty controlling her negative thoughts rather than trying to convince her that she shouldn't have them. She has them. She knows it, and nothing you say is going to convince her otherwise. However, when she expresses those thoughts, you can remind her that the thoughts are not necessarily valid. A child who says, "I'm so stupid" to herself fifty times a day needs to be reminded of the facts that dispute those thoughts. In order to break the habit of thinking "I'm so stupid," your child may need an alternative assessment that she could use to remind herself that her thoughts may not reflect the truth of the situation. For example, "I could have done better on that test if I had spent more time studying," or "I guess I need to decide which I want to do more, focus on my school work or spend time with my friends." This allows your child to have an active role in the changes in her thoughts.

Many depressed children have difficulty controlling their emotions or the extremes of their emotions. Let your child know that there are appropriate responses to joy and sadness, to disappointment and failure. When your child sees you sing with happiness over something joyful in your own life, or he sees you confront a personal failure with a plan to make changes to assure you won't fail again, he can learn to do the same.

Parents often play an active role in their child's treatment. So ask your child's counselor for specific strategies that may help your child. One such strategy is to identify and address the problems in the family that may be causing stress in your child's life. If you are having problems in your marriage, if someone in the family has a drinking problem, if you are suffering from depression yourself, or if you need to improve your parenting skills, seek help for yourself. We are in a better place to help our children when our own lives are in order. Additional sources about depression are included in appendix C.

Tourette Syndrome

Tourette syndrome (TS) is a neurological disorder characterized by involuntary, rapid, repetitive movements and/or vocal sounds (tics) that occur many times a day or intermittently for more than a year. The symptoms may increase or decrease in severity and may disappear for weeks or months at a time. Though these movements and utterances are most often termed involuntary, those with TS can sometimes delay the movements or utterances for a few seconds up to hours. Those with the syndrome often describe it as the feeling we have when we are about to sneeze.

These symptomatic movements and sounds are divided into two categories: simple and complex. As you can see from the list below, there is a wide range of behaviors.

In the simple category, symptoms might include:

- eye blinking
- nose twitching
- grimaces
- head jerking
- neck stretching
- throat clearing
- coughing
- sniffing
- grunting
- yelping
- shouting
- tongue clicking
- barking
- other noises

Symptoms in the complex category include more serious behaviors:

- jumping, touching other people or things, smelling, twirling about, and in rare instances self-injurious behavior such as head banging or lip or cheek biting.
- utterances which include out-of-context repetitive phrases (sometimes socially unacceptable comments or obscenities) including the repetition of another person's words or phrases

Most diagnosed with this disorder have symptoms in the mild category. Unfortunately, children with TS sometimes have other problems along with the disorder, such as obsessive-compulsive disorder, learning disabilities, or problems with impulse control. Forty to 60 percent of children diagnosed with this disorder also have attention deficit disorder. Difficulties with sleep, including talking and walking during sleep, is not uncommon. The disorder affects males two to three times more often than females.

According to the Tourette Syndrome Association, current research indicates Tourette is most often inherited as a dominant gene (or genes), and that the symptoms are caused by the abnormal metabolism of several brain chemicals such as dopamine and serotonin. Thus, a TS diagnosis is made by observing symptoms and evaluating family history. Children diagnosed with the disorder will have both physical and vocal tics, and they will have displayed the symptoms for more than a year. Often physicians use tests (MRIs, CTs, EEGs, and blood work) to rule out other causes of symptoms as there is no specific test to diagnose the disorder.

Because TS is so often associated with other problems, treatment plans must often address more than one set of symptoms. The parents, the physician, and the child (if old enough) need to decide which, if any, of the symptoms need to be treated.

The good news is that often children with TS do not need any treatment at all. Most suffer no significant disability as a result of the syndrome and do not need medication. Educating family members and teachers about the disorder and enlisting their support is still a major way of helping your child. Some students will need to have accommodations made at school, but there are many educational options available now for children with this disorder. If the symptoms are interfering with your child's ability to function at school, speak to someone in the school's special education department. Your child may only need the help of a supportive staff, but could also need tutoring, smaller classes, or adaptations in testing. Because your child will probably try to control tics as much as possible while with his peers, provide a loving, relaxed, and compassionate environment at home, where his tics will not be viewed critically.

For those whose behaviors cause a significant impact on their abilities to function, medications are available. No one drug can treat all of the symptoms of TS, and most have side effects. Drugs used to treat TS include clonidine, neuroleptics such as haloperidol and risperidone, and antianxiety medications such as clonazepam and others. Those who have obsessive-compulsive symptoms may be treated with fluoxetine, clomipramine, sertraline, fluvoxamine, paroxetine, and risperidone.

For children who also have ADHD, the stimulants normally used to treat the disorder may increase tics. For more information about specific drugs, including common brand names, see the "Treatment Options and Pharmacology" section of this chapter.

Remember, all medications need careful medical supervision; your child's blood pressure and pulse may need to be monitored on many of these drugs, and electrocardiograms may be recommended. Because TS symptoms range in severity among individuals and within individuals, adjustments in doses should be expected.

Though there have been no published studies of non-medication treatment programs for the control of TS symptoms and no long-term studies of their efficacy or safety, the Association for Comprehensive Neurotherapy (ACN) presents alternative options for treatment, believing some symptoms may come as a result of environmental factors including food additives, allergens, and others. This group provides information for families interested in knowing more about alternatives to medication. See the resources in appendix C for more information.

Because stress can play a part in the increase of TS symptoms, relaxation techniques and biofeedback may be helpful.

Also, psychotherapy may help children cope with the disorder and deal with the social and emotional problems that may arise. It cannot, however, help reduce or eliminate the tics.

Testing

The first step in getting treatment for your child is to schedule a thorough examination by your child's pediatrician to eliminate any physical causes for your child's symptoms. At that time, the doctor may choose to treat your child or to refer him to a specialist for further evaluation. When your child's behavior is having a negative impact in his educational setting, professionals at your child's school can help develop a plan to help your child. In some cases, psychologists, therapists, or school counselors will recommend that your child be evaluated through a testing process to get diagnostic information for pinpointing treatment.

Diagnosing these specific behavior disorders is very difficult. Scientists and doctors are discovering new information on a daily basis about the brain's behavior, but diagnosing specific emotional and behavioral disorders is not an exact science. Even all of the tests and checklists available are no substitute for good clinical judgment and the expertise of a professional. Many school systems have their own testing professionals who work with numerous children and have a great deal of expertise in interpreting the types of tests given to children. If you choose to select an independent evaluation, be sure the professional who will be testing your child is experienced in evaluating children. Ask your pediatrician or someone you trust for a recommendation. A competent clinician will use standardized tests, as well as interviews and diagnostic checklists, to help identify the disorder that is affecting your child's behavior.

When you decide to proceed with the testing, you should discuss the tests and procedures with your child. Be honest. Tell your child that you are concerned and explain why the tests are being given. The evaluation, whether done at a diagnostic center, hospital, or through the school, will vary the normal routine, and this can create additional anxiety. Alleviate this concern by explaining the process. When we don't level with children, they often anticipate something far worse than what is real. Try to be as relaxed about the process as possible. Tell your child that the testing will help you both determine the best way to resolve her problems.

Sometimes children try to fool an evaluator. Some children with behavior disorders deliberately lie to the evaluator. In fact, lying is a symptom of many disorders. Again, the skills of the clinician are critically important in figuring out what is true. The clinician will also gather information from other sources (school, athletic organizations, religious classes) to confirm or deny the information given by the child.

When Jared was asked, "How often do you fight with other kids?" he answered, "Never." Information from his school counselor indicated that Jared gets into fights every day at recess. A skilled evaluator will look at more than one measure before making a diagnosis or recommendation.

The first formal part of testing might be an individual intelligence test. Even if you are not concerned about your child's intelligence, it is a good idea to include this in the evaluation. An indication of your child's ability to learn and your child's strengths and weaknesses can give valuable insight into his behavior. The test can also be used to rule out other problems. For example, if your child's behaviors are more of a problem at school than at home, you may find that they are related to frustrations he feels when schoolwork seems too difficult. He may do anything to get thrown out of class so he won't appear "dumb" in front of his friends. On the other hand, your child's abilities may be so high that he does not feel challenged in class and wonders why he is so different from the other children. Attention problems can be recognized through intelligence testing, and recommendations for further medical testing may result.

In addition to intelligence tests, your clinician may use other diagnostic tests and checklists to help evaluate your child's emotional and behavioral state. All tests will generate scores that can be compared with the scores of other children who are the same age and grade as your child.

Intelligence Tests

The individual intelligence tests used most often are the Wechsler Intelligence Scale for Children-III Revised (WISC-III R) and the Wechsler Preschool and Primary Scale of Intelligence (WPPSI). The WISC-3 and the WPPSI must be given by someone who is specifically trained in the administration and interpretation of this particular test. They test general mental abilities and generate a verbal intelligence score, a performance, or nonverbal, intelligence score, and a full-scale intelligence score. They can also be broken down to provide useful information on your child's level of attention, language abilities, visual perception, and eye/hand coordination.

Another individual intelligence test widely used is the Stanford-Binet Intelligence Scale. It also must be administered by someone specifically trained in its administration and interpretation. It reveals general mental ability and offers intelligence scores, as well as information about verbal comprehension, nonverbal reasoning, visual perception, quantitative reasoning, and memory.

Rating Scales, Emotional Evaluations, and Behavior Checklists

The second part of the evaluation is usually a test or checklist to assess emotional functioning. The tests and checklists used in this phase are designed to give insight into how your child thinks, how he views himself in the world, how he sees himself in relation to other people in his life, his coping strategies, his defenses, and his emotional resources. It also looks at how his responses to certain questions correspond to criteria for the different behavior disorders as they are listed in the *Diagnostic and Statistical Manual for Mental Disorders*, fourth edition (DSM-IV), which describes symptoms of various mental health problems. The findings of this part of the evaluation can help determine a treatment plan. The specific tests and checklists are constantly being updated, but we are including the most common ones being used at this time.

The Goodenough-Harris Drawing Test must be interpreted by a trained psychologist. The skill of the interpreter is extremely important since this is not a standardized test with right or wrong answers. After the child draws a man, a woman, and a self-portrait, the examiner uses certain guidelines to interpret the features the child includes. Other similar tests use different drawings and are designed to give similar information. Useful information can be gleaned regarding your child's emotional state, his feelings about his relationships within the family, and his self-esteem.

The Bender Gestalt Test gives a score for visual motor ability (the child's ability to see a drawing and reproduce it), as well as indications about emotional states. In this test also, the skill of the evaluator in interpreting the results is very important.

The Thematic Apperception Test (TAT) and the Children's Apperception Test (CAT) are similar. The TAT is given to older children and adults, and the CAT is used to test younger children. The examiner shows the child a variety of pictures and attempts to get the child to talk about each one. The examiner is looking for themes that emerge to give an indication about the child's emotional state and concerns. The stories are then interpreted by the examiner, who uses suggested guidelines. Again, as there are no right or wrong answers, the expertise of the evaluator is critical. Because of that, the TAT and CAT are much more subjective tools and are sometimes misinterpreted.

The Rorschach Psychodiagnostic Test examines emotional functioning and personality structure by asking the child to respond verbally to ten pictures of inkblots. The responses are scored using various criteria. This test must be used cautiously with children who have learning disabilities because of possible perception, spatial, or language problems that could affect the way they respond to the inkblots. The Rorschach is probably the most objective tool, but it requires phenomenal training to be used correctly. Thus, most responsible psychologists who administer the Rorschach continue to receive peer supervision for many years just to keep their interpretations fresh.

The Sentence Completion Test presents the child with a series of unfinished sentences and asks the child to finish them. Here, also, the clinician is looking for themes that might indicate emotional problems.

The Child Behavior Checklist (CBCL) by Achenbach includes a Teacher Report Form (TRF), the Direct Observation Form (DOF), the Youth Self-Report (YSR), and profiles. All are paper and pencil, multiple-choice, and free response inventories that assess behavior and social competencies from the points of view of the parents, teacher, observer, and child. The different forms allow for assessment from more than one source and, thus, help to sort out what is actually happening with the child.

The Behavior Assessment System for Children (BASC) is more closely tied to behaviors described in the DSM-IV than the CBCL. This checklist is designed to identify a variety of childhood emotional and behavioral disorders and to help design a plan of treatment. These tests should not be the sole basis for making important diagnostic and treatment decisions, but the CBCL and the BASC are excellent screening tools.

The Connors Rating Scales are used in the diagnosis of ADHD. There are separate scales for parents and teachers. Doctors compare the child's symptoms with the criteria for diagnoses listed in the DSM-IV. Other rating scales work in a similar way.

The Continuous Performance Tests (CPT) is a computerized test developed to provide an "objective" measure of children's attention and impulsivity. In these tests, the child is required to push or not push certain keys depending on what symbols appear on a computer screen. These tests are designed to be repetitive and boring and have no resemblance to typical computer games. In order for a child to do well, he must be extremely attentive and not exhibit impulsivity.

Once your child has been evaluated by a mental health professional, the emotional or behavioral disorder is diagnosed, and a treatment plan is established. Sometimes a single counselor or therapist works with a child, but often children are treated by teams of professionals that might include your child's pediatrician, a psychologist, a social worker, a child psychiatrist, and a school counselor. They work together with you and your child to help overcome or cope with the disorders that are affecting her life.

Treatment Options and Pharmacology

The disorders discussed may be treated with a variety of therapies and/or medications. Though it is beyond the scope of this book to give a complete medical explanation of all types of psychotherapies, we are including in this section a brief explanation of common therapies that may be recommended for the behavior disorders in this chapter. Following the discussion of therapies, we present an outline of medicines that may be prescribed in the treatment of your child. Cheryl and I are not physicians, and this is not intended as a recommendation for treatment. All of the medicines listed here have side effects (some are serious) that should be discussed with your doctor. In most cases, medications will be used in combination with other forms of treatment, often for short periods to control symptoms that retard the progress of other therapies.

Psychotherapy

Most behaviors in this section may be treated with some form of psychotherapy—a treatment plan focused on improving a child's emotional or mental health. This type of treatment gives children emotional support, helps them understand their problems, helps them find solutions to problems by developing new skills, or helps them find effective ways to reduce their anxiety symptoms and elevate self-esteem. Most often, you will play a role in your child's treatment whether as an active participant or during discussion and information sharing sessions with your child's therapist. Certain disorders respond more favorably to one type of therapy than another, and that is a discussion you should have with your child's mental health practitioner or pediatrician.

Cognitive Therapy

The goal of cognitive therapy is to reduce or eliminate faulty, irrational, and/or habitual negative thinking. The goal of the therapist is to help the child change or control his thoughts. This type of therapy helps a child confront and change undesirable thinking habits.

Behavior Therapy

As the name indicates, behavior therapy addresses the child's behaviors or actions. The goal of the therapist is to help the child change the behaviors leading to the need for treatment. Therapists help children identify goals and develop the competencies necessary to achieve those goals.

Cognitive/Behavior Therapy

This therapy combines both of the above treatments and addresses thoughts and behaviors. This type of therapy helps children change their negative thoughts and behaviors. Depending on the disorder, this approach might include relaxation training and breathing exercises designed to help the child recognize and cope with the stressors in her life that are creating anger, stress, or anxiety.

Play Therapy

Unlike adults, children are often not old enough to talk about their problems. Children learn and express themselves through play. In this type of therapy, a child may use puppets, art, games, or play-acting to express his feelings through his own creativity and imagination. In this type of activity, a child can reenact troubling events in a symbolic way and can rehearse ways of coping as the therapist helps guide the child through ways of dealing with his thoughts and feelings. The therapist must be specifically trained in interpreting and understanding the message the child is giving through his play activities. This type of therapy is often used with traumatized children.

Psychodynamic Therapy

This type of therapy helps children and their parents deal with subconscious thoughts that may be affecting behavior. Using play therapy or talk therapy or some combination of techniques, the therapist helps the child to express the feelings that may be causing problems in her life.

Family Therapy

There are many approaches a therapist might take in working with a family. In most instances, the therapist works with the family as a group to improve communication skills and help develop problem-solving strategies. The therapist might also help parents develop more successful parenting skills and more effective methods of discipline. In this way, families learn to express their feelings and to develop new ways of working together.

Group Therapy

Therapists bring together children with like problems, and through talk and play, they learn the skills necessary to change their behaviors or to learn to cope with them.

Pharmacology

No medication should be given to your child without your informed consent. The doctor should explain what the drug is, why your child should take the medication, the alternatives to medication, the risks and benefits of the drug, the proper dosage, both the usual and unusual short- and long-term side effects, and how long it might take for your child to respond to the drug. Decisions to use medication should be made in collaboration with a physician—a family doctor, a pediatrician, or a psychiatrist.

Because you are in the best position to observe your child's behavior, you must monitor your child's response to the medication between visits with the doctor. You will also be responsible for seeing that your child takes the medicine and that he takes it in the amount prescribed. Overseeing your child's drug treatment is an enormous responsibility.

It is important to know what the medications can and can't do for your child. Current research shows that many of these disorders can be helped by medication. There are many different drugs available for children today. They help with the feelings of agitation, loss of energy, sad mood, sleep problems, concentration, guilt, and hopelessness. They can treat children with ADHD, ODD, depression, bipolar disorder, OCD, panic attacks, PTSD, separation anxiety, selective mutism, and CD. Medications are indicated for severe depression when there is an unwillingness to undergo psychotherapy or when the child shows suicidal tendencies.

Drug therapy is usually indicated when nonmedical interventions have been unsuccessful. Often parents hope for an immediate response when medication is prescribed for a child. However, most medications used in the treatment of behavior disorders take from four to six weeks before they began to work. Successful treatment often means starting slowly. In order to reduce the chances of negative side effects, most doctors will prescribe a small dose of the drug and gradually increase the dosage. If your doctor has recommended a drug treatment for your child, be patient.

The major classes of drugs used today are stimulants, antihypertensives, antidepressants, mood stabilizers, anxiolytics, and neuroleptics. All of the medications are designed to interact with the neurotransmitters secreted by the body.

Stimulants are most often used to treat ADHD and are the most widely prescribed medications for children. According to Dr. Jefferson Prince, physicians have more than fifty years of experience with these medications and when used in doses prescribed, they are very safe. Some, such as Ritalin® (methylphenidate), can improve alertness, concentration, attention span, and focus. Other than Ritalin, the most widely prescribed are Dexedrine® (dextroamphetamine), Adderall®, and Cylert® (pemoline). The most common side effects of these medications are decreased appetite, difficulty falling asleep, and irritability. Stimulant medications are often used in combination with other medications when ADHD occurs with other disorders like anxiety and depression. Sometimes a stimulant drug is combined with another medication if a child with ADHD has difficulty falling asleep.

Other medications used in the treatment of ADHD and tic disorders include the antihypertensives Catapres® (clonidine) and Tenex® (guanfacine). These medications may help diminish impulsivity and hyperactivity but are less effective in treating attention. They may also be used to aid sleep. As these medications affect blood pressure, they should never be stopped suddenly.

Antidepressants are used to treat depression and anxiety disorders and may be used to treat ADHD. The types of antidepressants used in the treatment of children may include SSRIs, tricyclic antidepressants (TCAs), and atypical antidepressants.

SSRIs decrease the brain's reuptake of the neurotransmitter serotonin. These medications have fewer cardiac side effects than TCAs (see below). SSRIs include Prozac® (fluoxetine), Zoloft® (sertraline), Paxil® (paroxetine), Luvox® (fluvoxamine), and Celexa™ (citalopram), and may be used to treat depression and anxiety disorders including panic disorder, OCD, and PTSD.

TCAs affect the neurotransmitter norepinephrine and to a lesser degree serotonin. According to Dr. Prince, they have been shown to be very effective in the treatment of ADHD and may have some use in treating oppositional defiant disorder, anxiety, and depression. A primary concern is with the safety of these medications as they affect cardiac condition and require monitoring with both EKG and blood level checks. Caution is also indicated as a one-week supply of TCAs may be fatal in an overdose.

There are other antidepressants that do not fall in any of these categories. These atypical antidepressants may be helpful in treating depression, anxiety, and ADHD. Some of them may act like SSRIs. The brand names are Wellbutrin®, Zyban® (bupropion), Effexor® (venlafaxine), Serzone® (nefazodone), Desyrel® (trazodone), and Remeron® (mirtazepine).

Lithium is a mood stabilizer and is used to treat bipolar disorder. It alters neurotransmitters, but it is unclear how it alleviates the symptoms of this disorder. Other mood stabilizers include the anticonvulsants Depakote® (valproic acid), Neurontin® (gabapentin), Topamax® (topiramate), Lamictal® (lamotrigine), Gabitril® (tiagabine), and Tegretol® (carbamazipine). These medications can have a variety of side effects and require careful monitoring of blood levels.

Anxiolytics are used to decrease anxiety. They are what we used to call tranquilizers. They treat panic disorder, agoraphobia, PTSD, and GAD. The following anxiolytics are addictive and should not be stopped abruptly: Xanax® (alprazolam), Ativan® (lorazepam), Valium® (diazepam), and Klonopin® (clonazepam). According to Dr. Prince, a nonaddictive alternative is Buspar® (buspirone), which may decrease anxiety.

Antipsychotic drugs or neuroleptics are used to treat tic disorders, psychosis, mania, conduct disorder, and self-injurious behaviors. Some older typical neuroleptics include Haldol® (haloperidol) and Thorazine® (chlorpromazine). Newer types of these medications are associated with less severe side effects and include Risperdal® (risperidone), Zyprexa® (olanzapine), Seroquel® (quetiapine fumarate), and Clozaril® (clozapine). These drugs require blood level monitoring. Very common side effects of these newer medications include increased appetite and weight gain.

This is by no means a complete list of drug treatment options. As the explosion of what we know about the functioning of the brain continues, new and improved treatments will become available or applicable to help your child with his moods and behaviors. As researchers look for newer drugs to treat these disorders, they also focus their energies on finding new medications that have fewer side effects.

Not every drug used in the treatment of behavior disorders has side effects and, depending upon the severity of your child's behavior disorder, you, your child, and your doctor may feel the side effects are tolerable in the short run. In many cases, the side effects go away when your child stops taking the drug.

Though there has been much interest in the herbal remedy St. John's wort for the treatment of depression, there have been no safety studies on children.

Consult your doctor for the most recent information on available drug treatment options for behavioral disorders.

CHAPTER 8

Everyday Strategies for Success

Children develop good behavior skills when we make practicing those skills part of our day-to-day lives. When problems arise, we can correct them with appropriate discipline strategies. But one of the most effective ways to help children develop positive behaviors that won't require discipline comes naturally from the way we live our lives and the way we treat our children. When we help our children feel good about themselves, when we act as positive role models, when we foster a sense of right and wrong in our children, we help them behave not because we demand it of them, but because it is the right thing to do.

Foster Self-Esteem

One of the most important factors in raising a well-behaved child comes from within the child. When your child feels nurtured, loved, and respected, he will feel good about himself. Children with high self-esteem have fewer difficulties at home, at school, and in social situations. In short, children with high self-esteem are well-behaved. That doesn't mean they never misbehave, but they misbehave under those conditions that would create difficulty for any child—when they are hungry, or tired, or feeling momentarily neglected, or under unusual stress. No child is perfect all the time, but children who feel good about themselves demonstrate their sense of well-being in the way they behave.

If we acknowledge that children who feel good about themselves have fewer behavior problems, what can we as parents do to help our children develop a strong sense of self-worth?

According to Dr. Stanley Coppersmith of the University of California, your role is critical in assuring that your child feels good about himself.

His findings, conducted more than fifteen years ago, still hold true today. Children with high self-esteem have affectionate parents who give them sufficient attention and who are consistent in their expectations and discipline. Families who give their children an opportunity to express their opinions and who discuss their expectations in a democratic atmosphere are more likely to have children who feel good about themselves.

In his studies, permissive parents and those who were inconsistent with their rules and responses, as well as those who were highly critical and judgmental, were more likely to have children who had problems with self-esteem.

In addition to providing clear and consistent rules, parents can help foster self-esteem in other ways. One particularly effective way is to catch your child in the act of doing something well. Too often we spend our time correcting what is done wrong. As a challenge, count the number of times you are critical of your child's behavior or performance during the day, and record the number of times you recognize your child for something he did well. If you are like most parents, your critical count will far exceed that of your praise. With just a little more time spent looking for the positive things, we can reinforce what's done right and give our children attention in a positive way.

Watch your child smile when you notice he put his clothes in the hamper, or shared a toy with a friend, or came home on time. Children love your attention, and if they can get it by doing something positive, they will.

All children have areas of strength. Find them. In a newsletter directed to parents of children with learning disabilities, Harvard psychologist Dr. Robert Brooks told parents to accent the positive: "There is not a person in the world who does not possess at least one small 'island of competence,' one area that is a potential source of pride or accomplishment."

When we make an effort to look for the good in our children, we always find it; and when we do, we feel great, too.

Make sure your child knows how special he is. When Mr. Rogers sings, "You are the only one like you, my friend," he is telling his viewers just how special they are. We need to help our children recognize the fact that there is no one else quite like them anywhere. They may have friends with the same interests, or brothers with the same eyes, or cousins who play the same games, but each of our children is an individual to be celebrated.

When children are young, they see themselves as we see them. Our response to the way they behave represents a mirror for them. When we present a negative face and response, they sometimes view themselves in a negative way. We can make such a difference by simply rephrasing our comments.

When we call our daughters "bad girls," they see themselves as bad people. When we shout, "You are so stupid," they see themselves as less than intelligent. We must challenge ourselves to provide mirrors for them that reflect positive images. Instead of shouting, "You slob, look at the mess you made in my workshop," you could say, "I like it when you put my tools back in the toolbox. I'll do it with you this time, and next time you can put them away on your own."

Ask yourself: If I talked to my friends the way I talked to my child, would I have any friends?

Sometimes children are particularly vulnerable and need a little boost. When mine were going through difficult periods, I would slip a note into their lunch boxes: *I'm glad you're my daughter. I love you.* Or *Smile. I am thinking of you.* These little affirmations can go a long way in the midst of a difficult transition.

Children feel good about themselves when they know their parents value their opinions and thoughts. Include your children in all conversations. Talk to them and listen to them. Ask them what they thought about a story on the news or about a specific event at school. We have all gotten the "nothing" response when we asked our children what they did in school, but if we said instead, "Tell me about the story your teacher read today," we might get a more specific answer. And then when you ask your child to tell you about his day or when your child does want to talk to you, *listen.* Most of us with several children and a multitude of obligations know we can do more than one thing at a time. I know that I can listen to my children and load the dishwasher, or listen to my children and browse through a magazine, or listen to my children and type—but young children don't understand that. When they want your attention, when they have something to say, they need your *undivided* attention. They need you to put down what you are doing and look at them.

Sometimes children are most expressive when they are upset or angry. They might come home and say, "I hate my teacher!" or "My soccer coach is a jerk!" or "I'm never talking to Jo Ann again." Children who storm in with these types of comments want you to pay attention. And while they need you to give them your undivided attention, they also need something else: They need you to listen to them in a way that will help

---

them express the emotions behind the angry comments. If you automatically say, "What did that soccer coach do?" you won't unravel the hidden message behind your child's comment. A better response would be, "I can see you are upset about something that happened during soccer practice." This opens the door for your child to tell you why she is angry or hurt. That's really what she wants to talk about anyway. When you take a more active role as a listener, you give your child the freedom and encouragement to discuss her feelings.

Many parents have regular family meetings to discuss the week's activities, to highlight children's achievements, to plan the upcoming week, to distribute household tasks, and to establish family guidelines and rules. When we respect and trust our children enough to allow them to participate in this type of decision making, we send them a very positive message: *You are capable of helping us make decisions. We value your opinion.*

Parents, however, still make the final decisions. We are the grown-ups, and it is our job. Children who know we accept our responsibilities will feel more secure.

Children have responsibilities, too. In most homes today, help around the house is a necessity. Children need to understand they are part of a family community, and as a part of that community they have obligations as well as opportunities. Even the youngest children can handle household jobs. When we provide them with an opportunity to contribute to the well-being of the family, when we provide them with tasks they can accomplish successfully, we let them know they are competent, productive individuals.

Self-esteem doesn't develop in an atmosphere of false praise. Be specific. They need to know exactly what they have done to please you. Instead of praising your daughter by telling her she is such a "good little girl" when she puts her plate in the dishwasher, encourage her behavior by telling her you appreciate it when she helps clear the table.

Children feel a sense of accomplishment when we stand back and let them tackle tasks they can complete. Nothing promotes self-esteem in a child more than self-sufficiency. School projects come to mind when we talk about giving children the opportunity to show what they are capable of. As teachers, Cheryl and I have seen children bring projects to school that they couldn't possibly have completed on their own. Children may need your supervision while they are working on class projects, but they don't need to have you do it for them. Step back. Let them show off!

If you have children involved in Cub Scouts, you have probably witnessed a Pinewood Derby, a race of handcrafted wooden cars. Many dads love this project. They make sleek, fast, high-tech automobiles. We have witnessed countless Pinewood Derbies. Though you would never get dads to admit it, most of them are not sure how their little boys would do if they were allowed to produce their own Pinewood racer. When you let your child complete his projects on his own, you send a silent message that says *I believe in you. I know you can do a good job on this. I have confidence in you.*

Like adults, children aren't perfect. When we expect them to be good all the time or to perform at their highest level all the time, we set unrealistic expectations.

My mother used to tell me, "I don't care what you do in life as long as you do it well." Though I'm sure she thought she was sending me a positive message filled with limitless opportunities, I sometimes felt overwhelmed with the challenge of always doing my best. It wasn't until later in my life that I allowed myself the freedom to try something I might not do well.

My foreign language proficiency leaves much to be desired, but I enjoy learning new languages. I'll never sing in a concert choir, but I love to sing. If I waited until I could do everything well, my life would be very dull.

We need to let our children know that it is important that they try. They might not get all A's or score the winning basket in the basketball game, but when they try, and when they improve, they feel better about themselves.

When a baseball player bats .300, fans consider him a star. Yet when baseball players bat .300, they fail seven times out of ten. Baseball would be a different game if we expected the stars to get a hit every time they approached the plate. If we expect our children to work toward improvement and recognize their successes, we must let them know their goal-reaching efforts have value.

Each child is unique—and not just in physical appearance. Be sure you and your child recognize those qualities that make him special. All children need to know we love them for who they are, not what we hope they will be.

Parents aren't perfect. Most of us are never satisfied. We often drive our children to be more than they are. If they are B students, we want A students. If they are the class vice-president, we wonder why they don't run for president. If they enjoy singing in the chorus, we wonder why they can't have a solo. It is probably human nature, but it's a habit we need to break.

Sometimes, in an effort to help our children improve, we spend a great deal of time trying to strengthen areas in which they are weak. If they are not reading well, we hire a reading tutor. If they don't make the baseball team, we drag them into the backyard to practice. If we spent as much time fostering their areas of strength, we would probably see our children truly excel in areas they enjoy.

Look for your child's strengths and validate them. Appreciate those things he does well. If she is a good athlete but not a great writer, celebrate her athleticism. If he is a wonderful writer but not a very good actor, don't send him to acting school unless *he* wants to go.

Because a positive self-image is so crucial in your child's development, make your home a haven of understanding and encouragement. With your affection, attention, respect, and acceptance, your child will develop a positive self-image, and he will be ready to learn his behavior skills from you.

Day-to-Day Strategies

Successful parents help their children set goals and offer specific strategies for reaching those behavioral goals. You can use appropriate encouragement and support as your child works toward that goal. As we mentioned earlier, we sometimes fall into the trap of expecting good behavior and then ignoring it when it happens. Be sure to reward good behavior with your attention. Attention is even more effective than praise. Show your child that she can get your attention for good behavior, and you will be well on your way in helping her want to behave.

Sometimes we can help our child reach a behavioral goal by breaking it into manageable parts. If the goal is for your child to clean up her room, break the job into small steps and praise her for each step. You might begin by having her put her pajamas away. When she's finished, tell her she did a good job. Then work on the toys in the middle of the floor. Once she knows that she can please you, she will work harder for that praise and attention. Identify what she has done so she is aware and will do it again. Focus on the concrete, not the abstract. "I really like how you put your pj's in the drawer" comes right to the point. It is much more concrete than "I like it when you are neat." Hard as it sometimes is to believe, children like to please their parents. When they know they can get your attention, encouragement, and praise with good behavior, they will work toward it. Attention for negative behavior only fosters more of the same. Strategies for coping with negative behavior are discussed in chapter 3.

All children benefit from making choices and learning from the consequences of their choices. Creating discipline strategies that help your children learn from their mistakes enables them to develop skills they will use for the rest of their lives.

Some children have more difficult temperaments than others. Any parent with more than one child can tell you some children are just more argumentative. Some children challenge their parents more than others. Some power-hungry children are frightened by a greater power; they actually feel better when they can exert their control. They seem to take a perverse pleasure in seeing a parent lose it. Parents say these confrontations often make them want to strike their child or in some way physically force them to comply. If your child routinely challenges your authority, avoid power struggles—you can't win. These children refuse to be dominated, so you can meet your discipline goals by refusing to dominate. Power-hungry children need guides, not bosses. As we mentioned in our discussion of causes, your choice of words and tone of voice will be critical in setting a mood that defuses otherwise volatile situations.

"Let's pick up your toys" will probably get a more positive response from power-hungry children than a challenging "Get those toys picked up now!"

Humor Helps

Parents and educators discuss authority vs. guidance with some regularity, but if you ask them what works best for them, they often mention another strategy instead. We don't even think of humor as a strategy, but as the old saying goes, laughter is often the best medicine.

Foolish fantasy can sometimes be more effective than repeated requests. Rather than asking your child to brush his teeth for the thirty-seventh night in a row, try having his toothbrush call him from the bedroom. In your best toothbrush voice say, "It's so lonely up here, and I'm so dry. I wish someone would come and put some water on my bristles. And I'm afraid I'm going to lose my job if someone doesn't come up here and put me to work." Foolishness usually pays off.

Sometimes we need to lighten up. Do those toys really need to be picked up right now? Will our effectiveness be undermined if our children don't load the dishwasher this minute? Will the cat starve if she waits until after breakfast for her food? We can sometimes postpone unpleasant tasks by providing some fun before they are accomplished. Read a book and then do the dishes. Play a game and then put clothes in the laundry basket. We can help children anticipate and carry out household tasks if we set them up with a pleasant introduction.

Share funny stories with your children. Let them know some situations can be resolved or at least managed with laughter. Let them see that humor has value and that you can enjoy a good laugh.

One counselor recommended collecting humorous parenting quotes. These quips are guaranteed to elicit a smile from even the most frustrated parent. His recommendations included Lionel Kauffman's "Children are a great comfort in your old age—and they help you reach it faster, too."

Harry Truman said, "I have found that the best way to give advice to your children is to find out what they want and then advise them to do it."

When my mother became exasperated with my sister or me or both of us, she often turned to a friend or relative and said, "Children! I'm glad I don't have any!" Even as a young child, I found the absurdity of her comment hilarious.

Form a "who can come up with the best parenting line" club with your friends. You will be able to make each other laugh even on the most difficult days.

Friendships with other parents can provide some of the best ideas for teaching children.

"I rely on my friends," one parent told us. "When we honestly share our parenting victories and parenting disappointments, we learn from each other."

Experienced parents offer the following advice: Think first, choose your battles, keep fragile objects out of reach, be a good role model, and share your values with your children.

When parents help their children develop according to a value system they believe in and live out, children are more likely to behave in a way that makes everyone feel good. Though our national values may be shaken by the behavior of our political leaders and sports heroes, there are always messages of hope as well.

Performing "random acts of kindness" is in, and the kindnesses come in all sizes. Newsreels of earthquake areas in California and Japan show countless incidents of courage and generosity. Young people at our school regularly serve meals at a local homeless shelter. When my mother was dying several years ago, hospice volunteers helped my sister and me through one of the most difficult times in our lives. This past holiday season, I lost my wallet. A seven-year-old boy found it and turned it in to the lost-and-found at the grocery store where I shop. Look around you. You'll see them. The kindnesses in the world can be inspiring. When we see someone behave in a way we admire, we need to remember that someone else *taught* that person how to behave. Someone instilled the importance of integrity and character, honesty and compassion, friendship and loyalty. Someone demonstrated how to hug and to share, how to praise and reach out, how to be fair and just, how to cry in empathy, and how to laugh with shared joy. That "someone" was probably their mom and dad. Now it's your turn to help your child develop a value system you can be proud of!

With guidance and encouragement, children learn to make their own decisions, based on solidly developed moral guidelines and the observation of moral role models. Discussions of morality sometimes make young parents nervous. Some feel disenfranchised by their organized religions, some believe their parents were too strict and associate their method of discipline with values development. Many didn't have role models and didn't receive moral instruction at home. Many don't know where to begin. Still, most young parents today are looking for a better way to help their children grow into caring, responsible adults.

They have their jobs cut out for them. The risks involved when parents ignore their children's moral development are greater now than ever. Children today face issues we wouldn't have thought of as children. Problems that our grandparents faced as they raised our parents seem almost insignificant today.

Families no longer live in the same community. Often they live on different sides of the country. Those nearby might not share a common value system. Religious beliefs have fallen by the wayside for many. Support systems for families are being reduced or eliminated. In many communities, older parents who no longer have young children don't want to pay for the social support programs that could help young parents. Many have washed their hands of today's issues, saying they are glad their children got through it all unscathed.

Not only are the support systems missing, much in society works to undermine the moral development of children. Violence on film, television, and recordings provide a grim picture of the morality of today's society. Many popular recordings promote behaviors that were unheard of when we were children. The continuing "me" generation drive for money and material possessions and the focus upon self-promotion pose great challenges in the raising of moral children.

Despite all that, parents today are ready to fight back, and though bringing up a child is always a challenge, most parents have the moral integrity necessary to raise moral children. An internal sense of right and wrong is essential for children. It is impossible to expect children to respond to any behavior strategy if they don't first care about their parents and what their parents think and feel. Children love their parents, and except for a few years in the middle of adolescence, they strive to be as much like them as possible.

Parents Are Moral Role Models

The best (and sometimes the most difficult) way to teach good behavior is by modeling it. We are our children's most important role model. That's both the good news and the bad news. Moral educators agree that children learn their moral behavior by watching their parents. The things you say enhance your value system, but the things you do form the guidelines your child will refer to when developing his own sense of right and wrong.

When we show our children how we expect them to behave instead of telling them, we become their role models in developing appropriate behavior. Because children watch us and the way we behave, our saying "Do as I say and not as I do" sends a confusing message.

If we expect our children to be honest, caring, concerned for others, hardworking, responsible, loyal, and kind, we have to structure our lives to provide living examples of those characteristics. We can provide positive role models for our children every day. We do it best when we deliver our message in a loving, caring, respectful way. We want our children to understand why we want them to behave in a certain way—why other people's feelings count, why we don't lie or cheat.

Though schools, synagogues, churches, and volunteer groups can help foster moral development in children, parents are the most important role models in their child's development.

You, and the way you choose to behave, will form the basis for your child's moral development. Take that responsibility seriously. You will make a difference.

The importance of parents as role models was poignantly displayed at the funeral of Rose Fitzgerald Kennedy. Eunice Kennedy Shriver remembered her mother as a role model for all the children in the family, and she said her mother's lessons were demonstrated in her actions. "Her acts of goodness were this child's classroom."

Your actions can be your child's classroom, too. Be careful. Like Santa Claus, children "see you when you're sleeping; they know when you're awake." Your best instruction will be the way you live your own life. We are all confronted with moral questions each day. The way we respond to them helps us judge ourselves at the end of each day. Now that you have children of your own, you not only can feel the internal joy of "doing the right thing," but you can also feel the joy of knowing you provided a good example for your child.

When we return a lost wallet, or notify a cashier when he gives us too much change, or admit we made a mistake, we are teaching our children by example. When we participate in community service projects, we tell our children those outside our circle of family deserve our attention and respect as well. When we back up our actions with an explanation of why we behave the way we do, it sends a powerful message.

Joan didn't have to tell her children that the elderly need our attention. Every week she visited an older blind woman at a local nursing home. When she first began her visits, she went to read to the woman. After several years, they developed a friendship that lasted until the woman passed away. Her children knew her visits to her friend were important. Her "appointment" went onto her calendar each week before any social engagement or other activity. She made an ethical decision each week, and her children watched her do it.

We must be on guard. When our children hear us lie to a friend or see us sneak through a red light or hear how we installed a splitter to get free cable service, we are sending them powerful messages. We are telling them it is OK to lie, OK to cheat, OK to steal. When we intervene instead of letting our children suffer the consequences of their mistakes, we tell them they need not be responsible. Someone will bail them out.

When we speak harshly to a service person, or we make irresponsible demands of a service person, we teach our children that we don't need to treat people with respect. The small acts can catch up with us and them in quiet, insidious ways. We want our children to be fair, to be kind, and to be responsible.

If you act as a good role model for your child, you have every right to expect your child to treat you and other adults and children with respect. From an early age, say please and thank you to your children, and expect them to say please and thank you in your home and outside your home. Children should address adults as Mr., Miss, Ms., or Mrs. First names should be reserved for those adults who give children permission to use first names. Do not accept disrespectful behavior in your children.

Disrespectful words not only hurt the parents, they threaten a child's sense of security as well. Parents who allow themselves to be belittled, degraded, or humiliated by their children leave them wondering who is in control. Children need to know their parents accept their responsibility and that they will provide stability and structure in their child's life.

Corporal Punishment
Is a Poor Moral Example

Some parents believe they can force their children to do the right thing, can "beat some sense" into their children. When they do, they deliver a message that says violence changes things. Violent behaviors may make your children obey, but they won't foster the sense of right and wrong necessary for them to make decisions when you aren't around. We want them to behave because it is the right thing to do, not just because they will get hurt if they don't.

As we've said before, when we yell at our children, humiliate our children, embarrass our children, or strike our children, we are telling them that yelling, humiliating, and hitting are OK.

"Moral lessons taught through anger and criticism yield only fear and resentment," say child development specialists David and Barbara Bjorklund. Children brought up within a violent family structure often bring that violence to their adult lives.

We wouldn't punish our children for a wrong move as they learned to play checkers, or if they fell while learning to ice-skate. Moral decision making is a learning process. Children get better with practice.

Foster an Inner Voice

As we provide examples for our children, we also take opportunities in their daily lives to teach them lessons in morality. Morality and child behavior specialists don't always agree on the age at which children can begin developing a moral sense, but they all agree that moral development comes in stages. Children enter the world with capacity for empathy. As we instruct our children, this moral capacity develops and grows. Children with good role models usually move progressively from a self-centered concern for what makes them feel good to a more mature concern for mankind. With support and with practice, they develop what behavior specialists Michael Shulman and Eva Mekler call an "internalized inner voice" that helps them not just to blindly obey but also to internalize standards of behavior they feel are important. Once children internalize these standards, they will behave in a moral way because they know it is the right way, not because they might get caught, or because it will impress an adult, or because their friends are all behaving that way, or because their parents will think less of them.

When should we start teaching our children the difference between right and wrong? Anyone who has watched nursery school children play knows even young children care about their playmates' feelings. Those of us with young children have watched with pleasure as our child tried to comfort a crying playmate by offering a beloved toy. Young children know the toy might make the child feel better. Teachers help them value the role of helper, too. Recently the father of a five-year-old told me how proud his son was when he got to be "teacher's helper." The family was proud, too. His mother went in to observe as he carried out his new responsibilities. The beginnings of moral development are there for us to see and nurture in young children.

Unfortunately, we have probably also seen them behave in less than desirable ways. We might see our children grab a toy from another child or push a playmate out of the way. Fortunately, even these troublesome moments provide teaching opportunities for parents. We can help our children understand why some behaviors are not just inappropriate but ethically wrong very early on. Our response to their behavior is a key factor in their ethical development.

Children want to please their parents. When they demonstrate hurtful, selfish qualities, we can let them see the disappointment on our faces. Once the situation has passed and children are in a receptive mood, we can talk about our disappointment in the way they behaved—not in them as children. We can help them understand why it is wrong to take another child's toys by asking them how they would feel in a similar situation. Young children are often very possessive of their toys, so they can understand without much difficulty the hurt they would feel if another child took away one of their prized objects. We can forgive them when they make the wrong decisions. They will get better at it with time and practice.

It is important that we point out to children that what they did was wrong. We need to explain why it was wrong. Then we need to help them come up with alternative ways to deal with troublesome situations.

Develop Empathy

Small lessons in empathy can begin as early as nursery school age. By the time children are about five years old, they can usually feel another child's pain. If we begin by teaching our children the Golden Rule, we are off to a good start. "Do unto others as you would have them do unto you" summarizes the empathetic way we want our children to look at the world. We want our children to feel pain when someone else is hurting, and just as important in their development of empathy, we want them to feel joy when other people are joyous.

Another standard rule in empathy training is "Love your neighbor as yourself." The rule sounds simple, but in reality, some children and adults don't have the positive self-image necessary to make the message part of their lives. In order to love our neighbors as ourselves, we must first love ourselves. Some children have such low self-esteem that it is impossible for them to even like themselves. Their self-loathing is transferred to all they meet. Whenever I see news clips of children who are in trouble with the police, this fact hits home. I look at those children and think, "These children can't possibly respect other people. They can't respect themselves."

Any instruction in moral development assumes a love of self and the ability to feel empathy. In any stage of ethical development, we have to foster our child's confidence, and we must provide them with opportunities to develop good self-esteem. As we mentioned earlier, you don't do that with reckless and undeserved praise. You do it by helping your child develop confidence in his ability to achieve.

Accentuate the Positive

We can foster our children's moral upbringing by providing them with rules, by presenting ourselves as role models, and by recognizing their ethical behavior when they make good choices. We can help them see the positive actions that occur every day. Though they are often buried on the back pages, moral examples are often reported in the newspaper. Find those that help your children see the good in the world. When a firefighter rescues a child, or a child tells the truth in a difficult situation, or a group of volunteers helps build a home for the homeless, point it out to your child. Discuss the moral values these people promote with their actions. Help them see that small acts of kindness can make a difference between someone having a good day and someone having a bad day.

Moral role models are out there. We just need to recognize them when we see them. We all know people who serve meals to the homeless, participate in fund-raising walks, volunteer at a nursery school, or perform some other act that benefits the community. Talk about those friends to your children. Let them see that acting in a moral manner is a way of life.

Under some circumstances, television can provide opportunities to discuss ethical behavior. Talk to your children about the way the characters behave on *Sesame Street* or *Mr. Rogers* or *Barney*. If your children are older, carefully selected situation comedies or dramatic programs can provide examples of strong moral character, or they can provide examples of the unhappiness careless behavior can produce. Discuss world issues with your preteens and teenagers. Let them know where you stand. Let them know why you feel strongly about your ethical opinions. Give them an opportunity to discuss their beliefs as well.

Literature presents excellent role models for children.

"Children don't hear the Bible stories, folk tales, or the tales of mythology that are so important in the development of morals," a middle school teacher lamented. "This void makes it difficult for them to understand many of the themes presented in the great works of literature."

Former Secretary of Education William Bennett believed so strongly in the power of literature as a source of ethical behaviors that he compiled *The Book of Virtues: A Treasury of Great Moral Stories*. Most of us heard these stories as children, and the words and deeds of the characters helped us develop confidence in our moral decisions. The fables of Aesop, the tales of the Brothers Grimm, the warnings in the "Little Boy Who Cried Wolf," the warning against greed in the story of Midas—all helped reinforce the values our parents were teaching.

Sometimes they provided additional little voices for us to call on when we were tempted. I can still hear Dr. Seuss's Horton providing a model of integrity: "I meant what I said, and I said what I meant. An elephant's faithful one hundred percent." I can still call up Madeline's courage: "To the tiger in the zoo, Madeline just said, 'Pooh-Pooh.'" The Little Engine That Could still speaks to me in moments of doubt. "I think I can, I think I can," it calls from the past.

The power of friendship displayed so movingly by Charlotte and Wilbur in *Charlotte's Web* is as important today as it was when I read it to my children. The importance of a strong work ethic is still alive in *The Little Red Hen*.

The words of the sages are still valuable today. Many contemporary writers also provide moral examples for our children. Ask your child's teacher or your children's librarian for suggestions, and read the classics as well as the new proponents of good behavior each day.

We can give our children those pearls of wisdom to store in their memory banks by recalling for them the sayings of our parents, grandparents, and other role models. Many parents used Franklin's "A penny saved is a penny earned" to instill the value of frugality in their children. My mother kept us from being too concerned with physical appearances and focused her attention on our behavior by saying, "Pretty is as pretty does." "Early to bed, early to rise, makes a man healthy, wealthy, and wise" helped foster good sleeping habits. More recent words of wisdom come from the film character Forrest Gump. "Stupid is as stupid does," he reminds us.

Most of us received the basics of our moral development through the Golden Rule and with the challenge of the Ten Commandments. Though it is unpopular in many circles today to talk about the value of religion in our lives, and the religious right and the religious left sometimes leave us bewildered, our Judeo-Christian roots provide us with structure, with expectations, with rules—and with consequences for breaking those rules. Organized religion continues to do that for families today. It can be a great source of strength and support in raising ethical children.

Churches and synagogues are not the only organized establishments promoting moral values, however. Volunteer groups are organized to help in every area of need. Habitat-for-Humanity workers build homes for those who need housing; volunteers staff hotlines and emergency shelters for abused women; hospice workers help families keep terminally ill loved ones at home. When your children see you involved in volunteer efforts, it lets them know you are willing to do what you can to make the world a better place.

Your children can become involved in groups that serve those less fortunate as well. Scouting programs often promote community service; school groups work to provide toys for children and clothes for the needy. When your child gives his time to service, he learns a valuable moral lesson.

Working for others fosters a respect for all individuals. We learn to respect those who need our service, and we learn to respect ourselves and to feel pride in our efforts to help.

In addition to finding ways to show our children the value of ethical behavior, we can work diligently to protect our children from undesirable role models. We can help them understand that the stars of violent action films do not represent the values we find important. We can help them recognize poor behavior in the sports figures they watch. We can help them by saying no. Just because your child's friends are going to see R-rated movies at a young age doesn't mean you have to lower your own ideals. When we explain to children the reasons why they are not allowed to watch inappropriate activities on the big screen, they might not like our rules, but they will respect them.

Just as we can censor their movie viewing, we can act as censors when it comes to television watching. If we act as solid role models for our children, and if we do all we can to foster a sense of right and wrong in our children, it is unlikely that television's message will replace ours as our children develop. We want to provide our children with models that support our beliefs, after all, and much of what is currently available on television does just the opposite.

Experts argue over the damage children suffer as a result of watching too much violence on television. But, as we said before, we haven't found an expert yet who thinks it is good for our children. When in doubt, turn it off! When you watch, select programs that support your value system. Limit the time your children watch television each week, and help them make sensible choices. Usually, when children have a limited amount of time to watch television, they will be very selective. Whenever possible, watch television with your children. You might be shocked to discover programs you thought were wholesome turn out to advocate lifestyles or philosophies you don't support. Don't assume your children will disagree with you. In a 1995 telephone survey by Children Now, children aged ten to sixteen described how television shaped their values. Seventy-six percent of those interviewed said television too often depicts sex before marriage. Some 62 percent said sex on TV influences their peers to have sexual relations when they are too young. Two-thirds said shows that portray hostile families encourage young viewers to disrespect their parents.

Children should not have televisions in their bedrooms. The temptation to watch programs they have heard about at school or from a friend might be too great. We can help them make good choices, but we don't have to provide them with unnecessary opportunities to make bad ones.

Help your children rediscover activities to replace television viewing. Play games, build models, read books, or get involved in sports.

Much of our job as parents involves making unpopular decisions. We can involve our children in the decision-making process and take their feelings into consideration when we make our rules, but ultimately the job of bringing up moral children is ours.

Many parents find it difficult to make these unpopular decisions. Many parents want to be their child's friend. Children don't need parents to be their friends. Friends are not responsible for their moral development. They don't set rules and provide discipline, they don't provide meals and clean clothes and a sense of security. Most children have many friends. Children can find friends anywhere—at home, at school, in the park. It's not your job to be your child's best friend. It is your job to love your child and to help him develop into a moral role model for your grandchildren.

Too often as parents we focus our attention on what our children will do when they grow up. Our efforts might be better spent if we concentrated more on what kind of people they will be when they grow up.

As teaching professionals Maurice J. Elias and Leslie R. Branden-Muller point out in a recent article in the *Middle School Journal:*

> ". . . the focus seems to be students' academic achievement, conveying the distinct impression that all that matters about children is their role as students and future employees. Amidst all of the emphasis on what kinds of 'world class' students our nation's schools should turn out, we run the risk of losing a more encompassing focus: encouraging the development of 'world class' *people.*"

As parents, we have the power to foster the type of behavior we will want our children to display as adults. That is powerful motivation for us to be the best role models we can be.

CHAPTER 9

Taking Control

Parenting. There is no other job like it. We love what we do, but it also scares us. Keeping our children safe—emotionally and physically—is an awesome task. It is a full-time job, and it can be exhausting much of the time. But when we do our job well, we and our children feel great.

No matter how well we do our job, however, our children will still misbehave. Children have been misbehaving for centuries. It comes with the territory. Even Socrates said, "Children today love luxury too much. They have execrable manners, flaunt authority, have no respect for their elders. They no longer rise when their parents or teachers enter the room. What kind of awful creatures will they be when they grow up?"

Society may have changed since Socrates' time, but we don't have to let those changes get in the way of raising well-behaved children.

If we want our children to have good manners, if we want them to respect adults, if we want their values to reflect our value system, we must rise to the challenge. If we want well-behaved children, we as parents must accept our responsibility.

As adults, we are in charge. Though we can't control all of our children's actions, we can set rules and consistent consequences that help our children feel safe and secure. When our children fall into bad habits, or develop behavior patterns we are unhappy with, we don't have to accept their bad behavior. We can hold them accountable for their actions.

If your child is having a problem, address it now. Don't wait for phone calls from school or complaints from friends. Don't postpone dealing with the situation. It will only get worse.

When we are disappointed in our children's behavior, we can look for the causes and address the behaviors with effective strategies designed to make a change. When we commit to a change, change happens.

We can nurture our children and help them develop a strong sense of self. With self-confidence, our children are less likely to get into trouble.

Most of all, we can be good role models for our children. They learn life's lessons from us; and when we provide them with living examples of the way we believe people should behave, we reinforce our words with action.

Remember, however: They are children. They are entitled to make a mistake every now and then. When we take time to recognize how well they behave most of the time, we can congratulate ourselves on a job well done. Take the time to give yourself a pat on the back. Most of us struggle with the responsibility of raising well-behaved children. We chastise our children and ourselves when things don't go as well as we would like, but seldom do we give ourselves or our children the credit we deserve when things are going well.

Review your successes with the following Parent Progress Report. Be generous with praise when you are doing a good job. Be realistic and honest when you see areas you need to improve. Give yourself a grade from A to C. Celebrate your A's. Write a plan for improvement for your C's. When you are feeling particularly strong, you might even ask your child to grade your progress and use it as a catalyst for discussion of how you both can change in order to improve the peace and harmony in your home.

Parent Progress Report

1. I am satisfied with myself as a parent. _____
2. I am a good listener. _____
3. I tell my child I love her. _____
4. I offer ideas to help solve problems. _____
5. I am consistent with discipline. _____
6. I make rules that encourage my child to do the right thing. _____
7. I look for positive behaviors to reinforce. _____
8. I set a good example for my child. _____
9. I model appropriate behaviors. _____
10. I laugh with my child. _____
11. I spend time alone with my child. _____
12. I create responsibilities for my child that my child can accomplish. _____
13. I set realistic expectations for my child. _____
14. I follow through on promises and consequences. _____
15. I say positive things about my child to others. _____
16. I am courteous to my child and others. _____
17. I look for ways to improve my parenting skills. _____

When you have reviewed your successes, commend yourself. As you refine your parenting skills, your successes will increase. Don't dwell on an occasional mistake. Just as they come with the territory for children, they come with the territory for parents, too. Don't let an occasional slip get in the way of your progress.

When you commit to a strategy for raising well-behaved children or a strategy for improving your child's behavior, you will succeed.

Don't forget to have fun. Raising children is a serious endeavor, but raising children is also one of the most joyous experiences in your life. Though the challenge of parenting can seem overwhelming at times, childhood is so short. Discipline your children, but also play with them, laugh with them, share in their fun.

We consulted "experts" when gathering information for this book. Remember, however, that those "experts" are parents just like you—parents who may have struggled through difficult moments in raising their children, but parents who know what it feels like to see their children grow into caring, responsible, loving adults.

With love, nurturing, and discipline, you will experience the joy of watching your children grow into the kind of adults you love, respect, and admire.

Appendix A

Sample Rules and Consequences Chart

Following is a suggested format for posting rules and consequences. Use this as a starting point for developing a list that fits your child's age, your discipline style, and your chosen strategy. Post rules for chronic behaviors that cause the most disruption and arguing in your house. If children know what is expected when they break a house rule, they will be less likely to argue about the response. In order for this to be effective, you must be consistent. We have included samples of a variety of strategies, including time-out and logical consequences:

Rules Examples for Young Children

Behavior	Response
Won't brush teeth	No sweets or desserts
Won't put clothes away	No clean clothes
Won't do assigned chores	Loss of a specific privilege
Forgets to take lunch to school	No lunch that day
Won't put toys away	Toys are removed for a day
Injures another child	Time-out
Refuses bedtime	Make bedtime earlier next night
Argues with siblings over possessions	Time-out of the object

Rules Examples for Older Children

Behavior	Response
Ruins someone's property	Repairs damage and is grounded
Injures another child	Time away from social situations for two days (first offense)
Misses curfew or time to be home	Loss of after-school privileges for one week
Refuses to do homework	No TV until it is done

These are just several examples of behaviors and consequences. Make a list to fit your own needs and circumstances.

Appendix B

Glossary: A Quick Resource for Problem Behaviors

Aggressive Behavior

My son has trouble taking turns. He overpowers other children, sometimes shoving them out of the way in line or taking toys away from them.

Aggressive behavior, pushing, shoving, biting, pinching, hitting, hair pulling, kicking, and so on are often a child's solution to a problem. Very young children often use physical force to get their way until their language development advances to the point where they can communicate verbally. Sometimes children use aggressive behavior to get your attention. Acts of physical aggression should be handled with a set disciplinary plan that separates the combatants and removes the aggressor from the attention he is seeking—time-out, for example.

If your child displays violent behavior against other children or animals, he may have a more serious disorder. See chapter 7 for information on oppositional defiant disorder and conduct disorder.

Anger

My daughter yells, "I hate you," whenever I ask her to do something she doesn't want to do.

Children express anger in many ways. Some children hit and kick (see aggressive behavior) others use angry words. Children need to be taught alternative ways to express their frustrations. If your child is falling into a pattern of angry behavior, first try to find out what is making the child so angry. Has anything changed at home? Is there a new baby in the house? Has your work schedule changed? Are you having marital problems? Is an older sibling making the child's life difficult? Is your child getting enough of your time and attention? Once you have uncovered and addressed the cause of the anger, the problem may go away on its own. If not, help your child learn to express her anger in a more appropriate way. Have her practice saying, "It upsets me when you ask me to make my bed while I am in the middle of playing with my toys." This type of response is more appropriate and respectful than, "I hate you," and your child will feel she has had an opportunity to express her feelings. Listen to yourself when you speak to your child and to others, and try to set an appropriate example.

Argumentative

Whenever I ask my eight-year-old to do anything, it turns into an argument. If I say, "Take out the trash," he says, "No." If I say let's go shopping for clothes, the response is the same. Every request turns into an argument.

A two-year-old uses the word *no* routinely as he strives to be more independent. An adolescent is in the middle of the same struggle. These are normal developmental stages. However, when your child's argumentative behavior begins to drive you crazy, it is time to look at the behavior as a problem. Parents are easily drawn into power struggles with their children. We often believe our children should do what we say and they should do it immediately. When our children refuse, we sometimes feel angry. Sometimes a change in our tone or manner of our request can diffuse a struggle for the upper hand. "When you get a minute, could you take out the trash?" might get a more positive response. See the section on power struggles in chapter 2.

Baby Talk

My six-year-old sometimes uses baby talk when my husband and I sit down to talk at the end of the day. She sounds so foolish and immature.

Baby talking is often an attention-seeking behavior. If you ignore your child when she talks to you in this way, she will soon get the message that the behavior will not get the desired result.

Back Talk, Sassy

My son is going through a very sassy stage. He talks back to me and to his mother, and his language makes us both very angry.

Most often children talk back to get attention. Usually, they are very successful. Nothing provokes parents like a wise answer from a child. Parents are right to expect respect from their children, but when they react to a child's back talk with shouts of their own, they give him exactly the kind of response he is looking for. When your child talks back, take a deep breath and in a calm voice say, "I won't listen to you when you talk to me that way." This is a little different from ignoring the verbal abuse. It lets the child know the language is inappropriate and lets him know he won't get a rise out of you by speaking to you in a disrespectful way.

Bathroom Talk

My daughter calls her friends "pooh-pooh heads."

This type of bathroom language is quite common in young children and typically appears at about four years of age. This kind of language is usually used with humor, not in anger. If you don't make an issue of it, bathroom language usually disappears on its own when the novelty wears off.

Bedtime Problems

Bedtime is always difficult in our house. My son whines and cries and sometimes even throws tantrums when it is time for bed. This battle is exhausting.

Children are reluctant to go to bed for many reasons. Some think that they are missing out on the exciting activities going on after they are in bed. Some resent the fact that older children get to stay up later. Some have nighttime fears (see fears in this appendix).

Most children need a firm bedtime routine that is predictable and comforting. Set your routine and don't bargain. Nighttime rituals can be reassuring to children and if properly planned can help your child wind down from the day's events. Set a schedule that works for you: bath time, brushing teeth, story time, hugs and kisses. Keep the routine calm and have your child in bed by the set time.

Bed-wetting

My son wets his bed every night. Even though we get him up to go to the bathroom before we go to bed for the night, he still wets the bed.

Occasional bed-wetting between the ages of three and six is not at all unusual. Many children have immature bladders or have heavy sleep patterns that prevent them from getting up to use the bathroom. Try to relax. When one of my children had this problem, my mother used to say, "I've never met a child who bed-wets in college."

Sometimes children regress in their nighttime control when under stress—the arrival of a sibling, for example. Sometimes physical problems can cause bed-wetting. If your child has been dry at night for sometime and begins to wet his bed again, consult your doctor. If your child has entered school, and the bed-wetting is creating social problems, ask your doctor for suggestions.

Biting, see Aggressive Behavior

Bullying

I hate to admit it, but my daughter is a bully. She picks on younger children, calls them mean names, and teases them unmercifully.

Most bullies don't feel good about themselves. They use their bullying behavior to elevate themselves. Unfortunately, this usually backfires. Nobody likes a bully. You must let your child know that bullying and teasing are inappropriate, but you must also begin to work on your child's sense of self-worth. See the self-esteem section in chapter 8. In the meantime, it is appropriate to remove your child from those she continues to tease and bully. If your child wants to have playmates, she will have to learn how to control her behavior. It may also be effective to have her apologize to those she has hurt. Sometimes it is very difficult for children to say "I'm sorry," especially face to face. Perhaps she could write a note or call her playmate on the telephone.

Cheating

I can't believe it. My son's teacher called today to say she caught my son cheating on his history test. He has always been a strong student.

Many believe only poor students are tempted to cheat. That's simply not true. According to recent reports in *Who's Who Among American High School Students,* 78 percent of the students said they had cheated. B.B. Houser's 1983 study of cheating showed that 22 percent of children begin to cheat in first grade. What makes children cheat?

When we place too great an importance on winning or on good grades, children are tempted to take short cuts. Examine your attitudes about winning and about grades. Sometimes we don't even realize that we are expecting too much of our children. Talk to your child. Be sure he understands that cheating is unacceptable. Set realistic standards. Explain the importance of honesty, and model honest behavior. If your child is having difficulty with a subject, arrange for extra help, and give rewards for the honest effort that goes into studying instead of a specific grade that is earned.

When cheating is part of a continuous pattern of lying, you may need to seek professional help.

Class Clown

I helped chaperone a class field trip recently and was embarrassed by my daughter's behavior. For her, everything was a joke. She mimicked the tour guide, she made fun of the exhibits, she repeatedly interrupted the activities with her antics.

While your daughter's behavior embarrassed you, it probably entertained her classmates. In all likelihood, they enjoyed her performance and looked to her for comic relief. Class clowns entertain for a variety of reasons. Sometimes students who are struggling academically deal with their frustrations with humor. They may not get positive attention for their academic achievement, but they are sure to get positive attention if they can entertain. Perhaps your daughter needs extra help with her classroom studies to help her improve as a student.

In some cases, class clowns are socially inept. They have difficulty making friends and are sometimes ostracized by their classmates. When they can provoke laughter, they feel part of the group.

Sometimes class clowns have attention deficits (ADHD) that prevent them from focusing for extended periods of time. Talk with the teacher about your daughter's behavior. If you suspect your child has a learning problem, talk to your child's teacher and to your child's guidance staff.

Try to find the cause of your child's behavior and address the cause, not the symptoms first. If your child does not have a learning problem and is academically successful, she may simply be using her behavior to get attention. Talk to your child. Help her discover alternative ways of getting positive reinforcement. Perhaps she could develop a skit to present to the class at an appropriate time. Maybe she can act as the teacher's helper. Tell her you will be working closely with her teachers to monitor her behavior. Weekly progress reports from the school will help your daughter get positive reinforcement for improved behavior.

Clinging

I have enrolled my son in the local kindergarten, but he refuses to leave me and won't go in the door unless I stay there with him the whole time.

Many young children have difficulty separating from their parents. Most have overcome their fears of separation by age five. Sometimes specific events trigger a child's anxiety. If a child has had an unpleasant experience, it is not unusual for the child to cling when reintroduced to that situation.

However, when clinging becomes routine for a child, the behavior needs attention. It is difficult for a parent to let go of a screaming child. Sometimes we feel as if we are abandoning our child in a moment of need. Try to let go of those feelings. Your child needs to learn to be more independent, and your role as a parent is to help your child. Advanced planning can help. Perhaps the teacher could have a special activity ready for your child at the start of the day, or maybe you could invite one of your child's classmates over for breakfast and let the two of them go into class together.

Separation can take place in steps. If you currently need to stay in the classroom for the entire day, begin tactical withdrawal. Let your child know you will be leaving at a specific time, and then leave. If you are anxious about your child's adjustment, check in by phone. Don't be surprised or disappointed to discover that your child is playing happily without you. Be sure to let your child know you are pleased that he is enjoying school.

If the child's behavior continues despite your efforts and the efforts of your child's teacher, your child may have separation anxiety. See chapter 7 for more information.

Fears

My daughter is afraid of dogs. She runs away from them whenever she sees them, and she is afraid to visit her friends who have dogs.

Fears are common in young children—fears of animals and insects, storms, loud noises, the dark, small spaces, water, or riding on buses or in other vehicles—are not unusual. As they mature, most overcome their fears, but when a child becomes fixated on a specific fear, you need to respect your child's feeling and take steps to help her overcome her fear.

Stephen and Marianne Garber and Robyn Spizman have written an excellent book on childhood fears: *Monsters Under the Bed and Other Childhood Fears*. It provides very specific advice on helping your child.

Most fears can be tackled gradually (as in the discussion of clinging above). First, find out exactly what your child is afraid of. Is she afraid of all dogs? Is she afraid of white dogs? Is she afraid of large dogs or small dogs? Maybe your child isn't afraid of all dogs, but only dogs with loud barks. Once you have identified the specific fear, you can begin to help your daughter learn to cope with her feelings.

It is important not to underestimate a child's fear. Help her develop a way of gauging her fears. She can rate it on a scale of one to ten, identify it with a spread of her arms, or let you know how "full" of fear she is—up to her knees, up to her waist, and so on. Ask her to explain exactly what frightens her.

Start by looking a photographs of dogs and watching dogs on television. Read stories about friendly dogs. Your librarian could make some suggestions. Role play encounters your child may have with a dog. Show her how to approach an animal. As your child becomes less fearful of imaginary animals, help her take the next step. Introduce your child to a friendly dog from a distance. Don't expect her to go close to the animal or to touch the animal. Just let her observe how others interact with this playful pet. Monitor her feelings by having her rate her fear level at each step along the way, and give her positive rewards and reinforcement during her progress. Encourage her to breathe deeply and to try to relax. Help her get closer to the dog at each session. Eventually she should be able to pet the dog. See chapter 7 for information about specific phobias.

Habits

My son bites his fingernails, sometimes until they bleed.

Many children develop habits that offer some comfort during stressful situations or when they are tired. Nail biting, nose picking, twitching, knuckle cracking, masturbation, rocking, and so on are activities children use to reduce tension. Sometimes, they become such an ingrained habit that the children no longer realize they are doing them. Most children outgrow these habits within a few years, and usually they begin to decrease by the time the child is five and continue to decrease until adolescence. It is important to remember that though these habits are annoying to parents, they actually offer comfort to the child.

When these habits continue beyond a reasonable age, parents may need to intervene. When older children suck their thumbs or practice other babyish habits, it interferes with their socialization. They might be teased or mimicked by other children. Parents need to help children find replacements for the habit. Nagging does little good and sometimes actually increases the stress that provokes the activity. Try having your child observe the habit in another child. This will help your child recognize his habit for what it is. Keep track of the situations that encourage the activity. If you can decrease the number of situations that instigate the activity, you can begin to break the habit. Help your child find an alternative to the habit. Maybe your child could handle a worry stone instead of biting his nails.

Hitting, see Aggressive Behavior

Hygiene

My son refuses to take a bath. He whines and complains whenever it is bath time, and unless I personally wash him, he doesn't get himself clean.

Why some children love bath time and play for extended periods in the tub while others refuse to get wet is a mystery to most parents. Some children don't like to bathe because they don't like to get water or soap in their eyes, some don't like it because it takes time away from more desirable activities, some just view bath time as a power struggle.

Once your child is old enough to be in the bathtub alone, getting himself clean should be his responsibility. Bath time should be a ritual. A time should be set aside for bathing, and the timing should be predictable and as inflexible as possible. Children can be encouraged to enjoy bath time if you supply them with bath toys they enjoy. For some, a small timer can be used to help them see just how little time it takes to bathe. Some children actually prefer to take showers. In some families, morning showering takes some of the stress away from bedtime preparations.

Basic hygiene challenges (washing hair, bathing, brushing teeth) usually respond well to charting. A small sticker can be applied each time your son does a good job of getting himself clean. Remember, his standards will not be as high as yours. Look for progress, not perfection.

Imaginary Friends

Recently my daughter asked me to set a place at the table for her friend, Tracy. My daughter doesn't know anyone named Tracy.

Imaginary friends are not at all unusual in the world of a three- to six-year-old. Rejoice in your daughter's imagination skills and set a place at the table for Tracy. Children use imaginary friends to try on different personalities and to practice social situations. Imaginary friends usually *disappear* as quickly as they appear. As long as your child has friendships and social experiences with other children, don't worry about her imaginary friend.

Interrupting

Every time the telephone rings my son comes directly to my side. He whines and pulls on my leg during the entire conversation, and I can't talk on the phone without his constant interruptions.

Children interrupt to get your attention. Have a basket of toys available for your child to use during "telephone time." Make sure he knows these toys are available only for those special occasions. See more about this in chapter 4.

Impulsivity

My daughter never thinks before she speaks or acts. She sometimes says the most embarrassing things.

Many children act impulsively simply to get their parents attention. Examine your child's behavior closely. If it stops immediately when you respond to the behavior, it is probably an attention-seeking behavior. See the attention-seeking behaviors section of chapter 2.

Sometimes impulsive behaviors are symptom of a more serious problem. Children with attention deficits and other medical problems may be impulsive. See chapter 7, "Getting Help."

Lazy

My son is so lazy. He won't pick up after himself. He won't do his chores. He just lies around the house and watches television. He's driving us crazy.

Very young children, five and six years old, might be lazy for a number of reasons. They may fear they will not do a job well enough, they may be feeling anxious about something, they might be tired or bored. You need to find the cause of their lazy behavior before you can address the symptom.

With older children, this type of behavior is often a form of rebellion, defiance, and on a more positive note growing independence. Still, children are expected to help around the house. Choose your battles and don't expect your child to march to your drummer. Avoid power struggles. The worst thing you can say is "Cut that lawn, and cut it now!" Engage your child when assigning chores. Have him give himself a time limit for the activity. For example, "I will cut the lawn before Friday." Adolescents need to take some control in their lives, and this type of interaction lets them assume the responsibility on their own terms.

Lying

My son lies all the time. He told his friends he met Batman while we were in California. We've never been to California, and he certainly didn't meet Batman there.

It is important to differentiate between this type of "wishful thinking" and lying. Many young children create stories to get attention, to be creative, or simply for their own amusement. Most young children engage in this type of storytelling.

Lying is something quite different. When children deliberately do not tell the truth in order to protect themselves or others or they lie with malicious intent in order to hurt others, lying becomes a serious issue. It is important that children understand the importance of honesty. Talk to your child about honesty and trust. Explain that honesty is important to you. Once your child understands your expectations, it is appropriate to discipline for lying. Separate the disciplinary measures. For example, if your child broke a window playing baseball in house and then lied about how the window was broken, you might take away his baseball for a period of time and then limit his phone privileges for lying.

Masturbation, see Habits

Overachievers

My daughter expects too much of herself. She wants to be perfect at everything. If she gets an A- on a test, she isn't satisfied. She is an excellent student, but we are worried about her.

An overachiever is one who performs above her level of capability. When students with average to above average intelligence perform at a high level, there is probably little to be concerned about.

However, when a child's intellectual potential is far below her level of achievement, there may be cause for concern. Many overachievers have parents who drive them for perfection. They set unrealistic expectations for their children and express disappointment when their children achieve at less than a superior level.

In addition, many overachievers put the pressure on themselves. They have an internal need to be the best at what they do—not their best, the best. Sometimes these young people become the success stories we hear about during graduation ceremonies. Unfortunately, they sometimes are the students who burn out before they have had a chance to fully develop.

If your daughter is performing well above what would be expected of her, help her set more realistic goals. If your child is bright and driven to perfection, help her find activities that balance her life. In either case, be sure she understands that you are proud of her achievements, but that she does not have to be perfect to be worthy of your love and attention.

Oversensitive

The typical teasing that would have had little effect on my older child is devastating to my younger son. He just can't take it. He comes home crying and says no one likes him. He's such a wimp.

Children can be cruel, and when they find a child who responds with sensitivity to their teasing, they sometimes take advantage of that child. Your child is not a wimp. He simply needs to learn to handle the tormentors. First, acknowledge the hurtfulness of their behavior. Let your child know that you understand his feelings and then begin to tackle the situation.

Your child needs to know that the children have come to expect a tearful response to their taunts. When they don't get what they are looking for from him, they will initially increase their teasing in an effort to get a response. Once your child has learned to ignore or diffuse their taunts, they will stop teasing him. Help your child develop a list of the taunts that he finds most hurtful. Role-play with him and help him learn to ignore those comments or to develop humorous responses to them. Be sure to praise him when he is able to better handle these situations and keep track of his successes.

Peer Pressure

We get a phone call from school last week. The vice-principal said our son was involved with a group of boys who wrote on the bathroom walls. He's never been in this type of trouble before.

As children get older, their friends and the opinions of their friends become more and more important. It is difficult for adolescents to stand on their own in the face of peer pressure. During this period, more than ever, children have a hard time being called a *sissy* or a *chicken* or a *nerd* when mischievous behavior gets started. Unfortunately, mischievous behavior sometimes escalates to more serious behaviors. Though we can never eliminate the pressure young people feel when confronted by their peers, we can help our children stand on their own by making sure they feel confident about themselves. Children who feel good about themselves do not rely solely on the opinions of others. See more about this in the section on self-esteem in chapter 8.

Poor Sportsmanship

My daughter is an excellent athlete and has been selected to participate on several "select" athletic teams—soccer and gymnastics. She usually does very well. Unfortunately, she is very critical of her teammates as well as the other competitors. If another child performs better than she does, she comes up with excuses. If one of her teammates has a bad day and doesn't do well, she is very critical. I don't like to see this poor sportsmanship in my daughter.

Sometimes young athletes expect too much of themselves and of others. They feel an almost compulsive need to win. Though we often expect high-achieving students, especially athletes, to feel good about themselves, that is not always the case. Some children feel their self-worth is based solely on their on-the-field performance. Let your daughter know you are proud of her level of achievement, but that winning isn't everything.

After a meet or a match, ask your daughter if she enjoyed competing or playing before you ask her how she did. Place the emphasis on playing rather than winning. Help her understand that everyone has successful days and not so successful days. Give her examples of things she could say to her competitors and her teammates. Things she can say when she outperforms them, and examples of things she can say when they are more competitively successful. "Thanks, I had a good day today. I guess the practice helped," or "Better luck next time. I know you were a little off today," are comments she can practice using. Be sure to praise her when she shows progress in her sportsmanship.

Running Away

I can't take my daughter shopping with me. Every time we go into a grocery store or into the mall, she runs away. When I call to her and tell her to come back, she might stop and laugh, but as soon as I approach her, she takes off again.

Young children enjoy this cat and mouse activity. They just don't understand why you don't find this game as entertaining as they do. Because running away in these situations can represent a real threat to your child's safety, you must let your child know that you take this seriously. Have a firm conversation with your child. Tell your child that you love to run and chase, but not while you are shopping. Explain that hand holding is required in shopping situations. If you hold your child's hand, you are in control. Praise her when she holds your hand. Though most of us don't like to see harnesses on children, some children require them for their own safety. If your child refuses to hold your hand, you may have to use a harness device as an alternative. Remember to play cat and mouse when it is safe—in your yard or at the local park.

Sibling Rivalry

My kids fight all the time. They are driving me crazy.

Because we love and care for our children, we expect they will love and care for each other. They do, but they don't always express it. As much as possible, ignore your children's disagreements. They really are their problem, not yours. Often children use battles with brothers and sisters to gain their parents' attention. When you ignore their disputes, you do not give them what they are looking for. As much as possible, stay out of your children's disputes. Let them learn to solve their problems themselves.

When children become physically combative, however, you need to intervene. Time away from each other is the most logical consequence of this type of behavior. See more about sibling rivalry in the sibling squabbles section of chapter 4.

Shyness

Whenever she is placed in a strange situation, our daughter hides behind us and clings to our clothes.

It isn't unusual for children to be shy in new or stressful situations, and some children are just more shy than others. Though you can't cure shyness, you can help your child feel more comfortable in new situations. Rehearsals can help. If you are going to take your child into a new situation, try role playing the event. Take turns with different roles. Shy children can also benefit by playing with younger children occasionally. This will give them an opportunity to take a leadership role and will give their a confidence boost.

Sharing

My daughter is so selfish. She won't share the toys at her preschool.

Young children have difficulty understanding ownership. For your daughter, the toys at the nursery school belong to her. Learning to share is part of normal development, and your daughter will probably progress naturally. In the meantime, help your daughter understand the concept of ownership. Examine items in your home. Point out her most beloved items—her truck, her doll, her soccer ball. Then, point out your possessions—your softball mitt, your jewelry, your favorite book. Help her understand that we all have possessions we value. Practice sharing. Let her use your pencils or your pen to draw. Have her return them at the end of a specified time. Explain to her that the toys at nursery school belong to all the children. Have her practice playing with a toy and then giving it to a playmate. Help her practice asking for a toy, rather than simply taking it from another child. With practice, most children begin to understand the process.

Stealing

I found a pair of pierced earrings in my daughter's room. She doesn't have pierced ears, and I knew the earrings weren't hers. When I asked her about them, she got very defensive. Eventually, she admitted she stole them from a friend's jewelry box.

Sometimes children just can't resist taking something they want. When children are very young, we can help them by defining possessions and the importance of ownership. Children can be encouraged to share their toys with others and to return toys belonging to other children after play. We need to teach our children that taking things that belong to others is wrong. We can do that by helping them imagine how they would feel if someone took one of their prized possessions. Have your daughter think about that. Then, insist she return the earrings. You might help her practice her apology, "I can't imagine what got into me. I liked those earrings so much that I took them from your jewelry box. I hope you will forgive me."

Stubborn

My son is so stubborn. We are always fighting to get him to do what we want him to.

Most parents understand that stubborn behavior is a part of a quest for independence. Just because they understand it doesn't mean they can tolerate it. Stubborn behavior gets to most parents. Most of the time, stubborn behavior is just a stage in the developmental process. To help your child through that stage and to maintain your sanity, there are several things you can try. Make requests instead of challenges. Avoid confrontations. Younger children need simple, clear directions, not commands. Look your child in the eye and say, "It is time to brush your teeth," or "We will start getting ready for bed in five minutes." As children get older, they consider any requests made of them as unreasonable. They develop selective hearing and refuse to hear anything they don't want to hear. At this stage, it is helpful to keep it simple. One-word requests, "teeth, bedtime, or homework," can be more effective than drawn out arguments. Older children do best when logical consequences are implemented. "Bedtime is at 8:30. When you begin to get ready when I remind you, you are ready in time. If you fool around, you will have to stop watching television and begin getting ready for bed earlier." Your child makes the decision and chooses the results.

Swearing (Profanity)

As I walked by the local playground recently, I heard my son use language I couldn't believe. We don't use that kind of language at home. I can't imagine where he heard such language, and I can't believe he is using it.

Younger children often try on "bathroom" language for size when they are about three or four years old and the novelty usually wears off quickly. Unfortunately, preadolescents and adolescents often make this language a central part of their vocabulary. If you can't imagine where your child heard such language, turn on your radio or your television. Children today hear obscenities with regularity, and we shouldn't be surprised when it enters into their vocabulary. Talk to your child. Let him know that you find the language offensive. Acknowledge that he hears other people use obscenities, but that for you and for your family, those words are off limits. With older children, privileges should be taken away if the language continues.

Tattling

My children are informants. They enjoy telling on each other and seem to love getting each other in trouble.

Sibling rivalry helps explain your children's actions. Examine how you respond when your children tattle. If you give positive reinforcement to the "informant" and discipline the transgressor in front of him, you are asking to have this scenario repeated over and over.

When your children inform on each other about minor offenses, and their motive for telling is spiteful, try giving doses of the same discipline strategy to both the informant and the transgressor. Tattling becomes much less desirable when it results in punishment.

Of course, when the motive is to protect the sibling from a dangerous activity and from harm, the situation is entirely different. In this case, you should thank your child for the courage to come to you with the information. When you discipline his sibling it should be out of the hearing and sight of his brother.

Teasing, see Bullying

Temper Tantrums

Whenever I tell my daughter to do something she doesn't want to do or tell her not to do something she wants to do, she throws herself on the floor and kicks her feet. When I try to pick her up to comfort her, she makes her body stiff and holds her breath.

Most children have temper tantrums at some point in the growing up process. Most have tantrums to get their parents' attention. Because this is an attention-seeking behavior, the worst thing you can do is give your child what she is looking for. Instead, walk away from her. If she is disturbing other people with her tantrum, pick her up and move her to a more private spot and then ignore her. She will soon learn that tantrums will not get the desired response.

Victims, see Oversensitive

Underachievers

My son has above average standardized test scores, yet he only does average work in school. His teacher says he is capable of more.

Have your child's guidance department give your child more individualized tests to confirm the standardized test scores. If he is indeed performing below the expected levels, and he has no learning disability contributing to his underachievement, help him set levels of expectation. Just because he is capable of A work, doesn't mean he will do A work. Look instead for improvement. If he is now getting Cs, perhaps he might set his goal at a B-. Praise the improvement, and help him set new goals.

In some situations, your child may feel it is socially unacceptable to excel. It is unfortunate, but some children believe doing well in school makes them a nerd. In that case, you can use the strategies to develop self-esteem so they will be less influenced by the beliefs of their peers.

If this performance is new for your child, it may have to do with the teacher's teaching style. Discuss this with your child's teacher and the guidance counselor.

Whining

My son's whining is driving me crazy. I don't even like to listen to his voice any more.

Children whine when they are tired, when they are hungry, when they are bored, and often when they want to get attention. When children whine because they are hungry, or tired, or bored, the solutions are relatively easy to address. When they whine to get your attention, the problem is a little more difficult. Help your child understand what you mean by whining. Role-play a whining voice and tell him you will not respond to whining. If he whines, don't respond. You supply your child with an alternative when you explain that you will only answer when he uses an appropriate voice. This type of behavior responds well to charting. See the charting section of chapter 3.

Appendix C

National Agencies, Hotlines, and Resources

The following agencies, hotlines, and recommended readings can offer further information and support for parents of children with mental, emotional, or behavioral disorders.

Abuse

Parents Anonymous
675 West Foothill Boulevard, Suite 220
Claremont, CA 91711
909-621-6184
http://www.parentsanonymous-natl.org

National Child Abuse Hotline
1-800-4-A-CHILD (1-800-422-4453)

Alcohol and Drug Abuse

Al-Anon/Alateen
1600 Corporate Landing
Virginia Beach, VA 23454
http://www.al-anon.alateen.org/

Alcoholics Anonymous
Box 459, Grand Central Station
New York, NY 10163
212-870-3400
www.alcoholics-anonymous.org

Families Anonymous
Box 3475
Culver City, CA 90231
http://home.earthlink.net/~famanon/index.html

National Institute on Drug Abuse
6001 Executive Blvd., RM 5274 MSC 9581
Bethesda, MD 20892-9581
http://www.nida.nih.gov/

U.S. Department of Health and Human Services
Center for Substance Abuse Treatment
National Helpline
1-800-662-HELP (treatment referrals)

Recommended Reading

Growing Up Drug-Free: A Parent's Guide to Prevention (Available from: Safe and Drug Free Schools Program, ED Pubs, P.O. Box 1398, Jessup, MD 20794-1398; 1-887-4-ED-PUBS).

Kuhn, Cynthia, Ph.D., Scott Swartzwelder, Ph.D, and Wilkie Wilson, Ph.D. *Buzzed: The Straight Facts About the Most Used and Abused Drugs from Alcohol to Ecstasy.* New York: W. W. Norton & Co., 1998.

Milhorn, H. Thomas, Jr. *Drug and Alcohol Abuse: The Authoritative Guide for Parents, Teachers, and Counselors.* New York: Plenum Press, 1994.

U.S. Department of Education Web Site. http://www.ed.gov/offices/OESE/SDFS/parents_guide

Anxiety Disorders

Find a support group, either at your child's school, through your community mental health center, or online. The following agencies can also offer support and information.

American Academy of Child and Adolescent Psychiatry
3615 Wisconsin Avenue NW
Washington, DC 20016
202-966-7300 (for the Council of Child and Adolescent
    Psychiatry nearest you)
http://www.aacap.org

Anxiety Disorders Association of America
Suite 100
1119 Parklawn Drive
Rockville, MD 20852-2624
http://www.adaa.org/

National Institute of Mental Health Panic Campaign
Room 7C-05
5600 Fishers Lane
Rockville, MD 20857
1-800-64-PANIC

National Institute of Mental Health Web Site
Anxiety Disorders Education Program
Division of Communications
5600 Fishers Lane
Rockville, MD 20857
301-443-3673
http://www.nimh.nih.gov/anxiety/index.htm

Obsessive-Compulsive Foundation, Inc.
P.O. Box 70
Milford, CT 06460-0070
203-878-5669

The Selective Mutism Foundation, Inc.
P.O. Box 13133
Sissonville, WV 25360-0133

Recommended Reading

Carter, Rosalyn, with Susan K. Golant. *Helping Someone with Mental Illness: A Compassionate Guide for Family, Friends and Caregivers*. New York: Times Books, 1998.

Gravitz, Herbert L., Ph.D. *Obsessive Compulsive Disorder: New Help for the Family*. San Luis Obispo, Calif.: Healing Visions Press, 1998.

March, John S., ed. *Anxiety Disorders in Children and Adolescents*. New York: Guilford Press, 1995.

March, John S., M.D., M.P.H., and Karen Mulle, B.S.N., M.T.S., M.S.W. *OCD in Children and Adolescents*. New York: Guilford Press, 1998.

Miller, Thomas W., ed. *Children of Trauma : Stressful Life Events and Their Effects on Children and Adolescents*. Madison, Conn.: International Universities Press, 1998.

Silverman, Wendy K., and William M. Kurtines. *Anxiety and Phobic Disorders: A Pragmatic Approach*. New York: Plenum Press, 1996.

Depression

American Academy of Child and Adolescent Psychiatry
3615 Wisconsin Avenue NW
Washington, DC 20016
1-800-333-7636
http://www.aacap.org/index.htm

Depression Awareness, Recognition, and Treatment (D/ART)
5600 Fisher Lane
Rockville, MD 20857
1-800-421-4211
http://www.nimh.nih.gov/dart/index.htm

National Depressive and Manic-Depressive Association
Suite 501
730 North Franklin Street
Chicago, IL 60610-3526
http://www.ndmda.org

Recommended Reading

Hallowell, E. M. *When You Worry About the Child You Love: Emotional and Learning Problems in Children*. New York: Fireside, 1996.

Miller, Jeffrey A., Ph.D. *The Childhood Depression Sourcebook*. Los Angeles: Lowell House, 1999.

Disruptive Behavior Disorders

American Academy of Child and Adolescent Psychiatry
3615 Wisconsin Avenue NW
Washington, DC 20016
1-800-333-7636
http://www.aacap.org/index.htm

National Mental Health Association
1021 Prince Street
Alexandria, VA 22312
1-800-969-NMHA
http://www.nmha.org

Oppositional Defiant Support Group
http://www.conductdisorders.com
(online only)

Recommended Reading

Bodenhamer, Gregory. *Back in Control*. Upper Saddle River, N.J.: Prentice Hall, 1992.

————. *Parent in Control*. New York: Fireside, 1995.

Flick, Grad L., Ph.D., and Harvey C. Parker. *Power Parenting for Children With ADD/ADHD: A Practical Parent's Guide for Managing Difficult Behaviors*. West Nyack, N.J.: Center for Applied Research in Education, 1996.

Gollant, Mitch, and Donna G. Corwin. *The Challenging Child*. New York: Berkley Publishing Group, 1995.

Keck, Gregory C., and Regina M. Kupecky. *Adopting the Hurt Child: Hope for Families with Special-Needs Kids: A Guide for Parents and Professionals*. Colorado Springs: Pinon Press, 1998.

Lynn, George T. *Survival Strategies for Parenting your ADD Child: Dealing with Obsessions, Compulsions, Depressions, Explosive Behavior and Rage*. Grass Valley, Calif.: Underwood Books, 1996.

Samenow, Stanton E. *Before It's Too Late*. New York: Times Books, 1989.

Pharmacology

Recommended Reading

Editors of Consumer's Guide. *Children's Prescription Drugs: A Parent's Guide to the Most Commonly Recommended Drugs for Children*. New York: Signet, 1997.

Gorman, Jack M., M.D. *The Essential Guide to Psychiatric Drugs*. New York: St. Martin's Press, 1998.

Home-Health Center
http://home.health-center.com

Tourette Syndrome

Association for Comprehensive NeuroTherapy
1128 Royal Palm Beach Boulevard, #283
Royal Palm Beach, FL 33411
561-798-0472
http://www.latitudes.org

Tourette Syndrome Association
42-40 Bell Boulevard
Bayside, NY 11361-2820
718-224-2999
http://neuro-www2.mgh.harvard.edu/tsa/tsamain.nclk

Recommended Reading

Eisenreich, Jim. *Children with Tourette Syndrome: A Parent's Guide*. Edited by Tracy Haerle. Rockville, Md.: Woodbine House, 1992.

Handler, Lowell. *Twitch and Shout: A Touretter's Tale*. New York: E. P. Dutton, 1998.

Recommended Reading for All of the Above Disorders

Koplewicz, Harold S., M.D. *It's Nobody's Fault: New Hope and Help for Difficult Childen and Their Parents*. New York: Times Books, 1996.

Appendix D

Bibliography

Ames, Louise. *Raising Good Kids: A Developmental Approach to Discipline*. Rosemont, N.J.: Modern Learning Press, 1992.

Baldrige, Letitia. *Letitia Baldrige's More Than Manners! Raising Today's Kids to Have Kind Manners and Good Hearts*. New York: Scribner, 1997.

Bennett, William J., ed. *The Book of Virtues*, New York: Simon & Schuster, 1993.

Bernstein, Gail A., M.D., and Joan Kinlan, M.D., et al. "Summary of Practice Parameters for the Assessment and Treatment of Children and Adolescents with Anxiety Disorder," American Academy of Child and Adolescent Psychiatry. Available online at: http://www.aacaplorg/clinical/Anxtysum.htm (February 1, 1999).

Blume, Judy. *Letters to Judy: What Your Kids Wish They Could Tell You*. New York: Putnam, 1986.

Bjorklund, David F., and Barbara R. Bjorklund. *Parents Book of Discipline*. New York: Ballantine, 1990.

Coles, Robert. *The Moral Life of Children*. Boston: Houghton Mifflin, 1986.

Coloroso, Barbara. *Kids Are Worth It: Giving Your Child the Gift of Inner Discipline*. New York: William Morrow, 1994.

"Depression Research at the National Institute of Mental Health (Fact Sheet)," National Institute of Mental Health. Available online at: http://www.nimh.nih.gov/publicat/depresfact.htm (March 30, 1999).

"Depressive Illness: Treatments Bring New Hope," National Institute of Mental Health. Available online at: http://

www.nimh.nih.gov/dart1/newhope/causes.htm (March 30, 1999).

Diagnostic and Statistical Manual of Mental Disorders: DSM-IV, Fourth Edition. Washington, D.C.: American Psychiatric Association, 1994.

Dicky, Marilyn. "Anxiety Disorders." National Institute of Mental Health (NIH Publication No. 97-3870), 1997.

———. "Decade of the Brain." National Institute of Mental Health (NIH Publication No. 94-3879), 1994.

Dinkmeyer, Don, and Gary D. McKay. *The Parent's Handbook: STEP Systematic Training for Effective Parenting.* Circle Pines, Minn.: American Guidance Service, 1988.

———. *Raising a Responsible Child.* New York: Simon & Schuster, 1973.

Dreikurs, Rudolf, M.D., with Vicki Soltz, R.N. *Children: The Challenge.* New York: Plume, 1991.

Eckman, Paul. *Why Kids Lie: How Parents Can Encourage Truthfulness.* New York: Scribner, 1989.

Elias, Maurice J., and Leslie R. Branden-Muller. "Social and Life Skills Development during the Middle School Years: An Emerging Perspective." *Middle School Journal* (January, 1994): 3–7.

Garber, Stephen, Marianne Garber, and Robyn Spizman. *Good Behavior Made Easy Handbook.* Glastonbury, Conn.: Great Pond Publishing, 1992.

———. *Monsters Under the Bed and Other Childhood Fears.* New York: Villard, 1993.

Ginsburg, Golda S., Annette M. LaGreca, and Wendy K. Silverman. "Social Anxiety in Children with Anxiety Disorders: Relation with Social and Emotional Functioning." *Journal of Abnormal Child Psychology* 26, no. 3 (June 1998). Available from Infotrac SearchBank Database online at: http://www.searchbank.com/searchbank/mlin_n_remote.

Hallowell, Edward M., M.D., and John J. Ratcy, M.D. *Driven to Distraction: Recognizing and Coping with Attention Deficit Disorder from Childhood through Adulthood.* New York: Simon and Schuster, 1995.

Kingma, Daphne Rose, et al. *Random Acts of Kindness.* Berkeley: Conari Press, 1993.

Levy, Ted. "Planning for More Effective Parent Conferences." *Middle School Journal.* (September, 1994): 49–51.

"Little Evidence Found of Incorrect Diagnosis or Overprescription for ADHD: Abuse of Stimulants Not Seen as Major Problem at This Time." *Journal of the American Medical Association.* Available online at: http://www.add.org/content/treatment/jama.htm (April 2, 1999).

Long, Phillip W. "Children's Conduct Disorders." *The Harvard Medical School Mental Health Letter.* Available online at: http://www.mentalhealth.com/mag1/p5h-cond.html (March 1, 1999).

McCullough, Virginia E. *Testing and Your Child: What You Should Know about 150 of the Most Common Medical, Educational, and Psychological Tests.* New York: Plume, 1992.

Miller Jeffrey A., Ph.D. *The Childhood Depression Sourcebook.* Los Angeles: Lowell House, 1999.

Neuwirth, Sharyn, M.Ed. "Attention Deficit Hyperactivity Disorder: Decade of the Brain." National Institute of Mental Health (NIH Publication No. 94-3572), 1994.

Nowicki, Stephen, and Marshall Duke. *Helping a Child Who Doesn't Fit In.* Atlanta: Peachtree, 1992.

Reuben, Steven Carr. *Children of Character: Leading Your Children to Ethical Choices in Everyday Life, A Parent's Guide.* Edited by Marlene Canter and Carol Provisor. Santa Monica, Calif.: Lee Canter & Assoc., 1997.

———. *Raising Ethical Children: Ten Keys to Helping Your Children Become Moral and Caring.* Roseville City, Calif.: Prima Publishing, 1994.

Roiphe, Herman, M.D., and Anne Roiphe. *Your Child's Mind: The Complete Guide to Infant and Child Emotional Well-Being*. New York: St. Martin's, 1985.

Samalin, Nancy, with Martha M. Jablow. *Positive Discipline That Works*. New York: Penguin, 1998.

"SAMHSA Office of Applied Studies: Substance Abuse and Mental Health Statistics." Available online at: http://www.samhsa.gov/OAS/OASFTP/HTM (June 17, 1999).

Schulman, Michael, and Eva Mekler. *Bringing Up a Moral Child: A New Approach for Teaching Your Child to Be Kind, Just, and Responsible*. New York: Doubleday, 1994.

Shure, Myrna. *Raising a Thinking Child*. New York: Pocket Books, 1996.

Sommers-Flanagan, John, and Rita Sommers-Flanagan. "Assessment and Diagnosis of Conduct Disorder." *Journal of Counseling & Development* 76, no. 2 (Spring 1998): 189–97. ERIC No. EJ568405. Available from EBSCOhost subscriber database online at: http://gw1.epnet.com/ehost.asp?key=kgO2NFG.

Stock, Gregory. *The Kids' Book of Questions*. New York: Workman Publishing, 1988.

"Structuring Schools for Success: A Focus on Attention Deficits." Brochure. Commonwealth of Massachusetts, Department of Education, 1994.

"Tourette Syndrome." National Institute of Neurological Disorders and Stroke (NIH Publication No. 95-2163), 1995.

Tuttle, Cheryl Gerson, and Penny Paquette. *Parenting a Child with a Learning Disability*. New York: Doubleday, 1995.

White, Burton. *The First Three Years of Life*. New York: Doubleday, 1991.

Wyckoff, Jerry L., and Barbara C. Unell. *How to Discipline Your Six to Twelve Year Old . . . Without Losing Your Mind*. New York: Doubleday, 1991.

Index